C R O C H

A Passion For Pineapples™

General Information

Many of the products used in this pattern book can be purchased from local craft, fabric and variety stores or from the Annie's Attic Needlecraft Catalog *(see page 55 for catalog information)*.

Pineapples & Pearls

Design by Maggie Petsch

SKILL LEVEL

  INTERMEDIATE

FINISHED SIZE
7¾ inches square, including Border

MATERIALS
- Coats Opera crochet cotton size 5 (50 grams per ball):
   2 balls #500 white
- Crochet cotton size 30:
   Small amount white
- Kreinik blending filament (55 yds per spool):
   5 spools #032-BF pearl
- Size 10/1.15mm steel crochet hook
- Size B/1/2.25mm crochet hook or size needed to obtain gauge
- Sewing needle
- White sewing thread
- ¼ yd white fabric
- 9 inch white all-purpose zipper
- Pearl beads:
   ⅛ inch: 90
   3/16 inch: 8
   1/16 inch: 9
- Commercial fabric stiffener
- Small paintbrush

GAUGE
Rnds 1–5 of side = 1½ inches in diameter

PATTERN NOTES
Purse is worked with one strand crochet cotton and one strand blending filament held tog throughout unless otherwise stated.

Size 30 thread and size 10 crochet hook are used for zipper pull only.

SPECIAL STITCHES
Shell: (3 dc, ch 2, 3 dc) in indicated ch sp or st.

Beginning shell (beg shell): (Ch 3–*counts as first dc*, 2 dc, ch 2, 3 dc) in indicated ch sp or st.

Cluster (cl): Yo, insert hook in indicated st or ch sp, yo, pull lp through, yo, pull through 2 lps on hook, [yo, insert hook in same st or ch sp, yo, pull lp through, yo, pull through 2 lps on hook] twice, yo, pull through all lps on hook.

V-stitch (V-st): (Dc, ch 3, dc) in indicated ch sp or st.

Picot: Ch 2, sl st in second ch from hook.

Single crochet cord (sc cord): Ch 2, sc in second ch from hook, twist work ½ turn away from you, insert hook under single vertical strand at top of work, yo, pull up a lp, complete sc, [twist work ½ turn away from you, insert hook under double vertical strand at top of work, yo, pull up lp, complete sc] for desired length.

INSTRUCTIONS
SIDE
Make 2.

Rnd 1 (RS): Ch 2, 8 sc in second ch from hook, join with sl st in beg sc. *(8 sc)*

Rnd 2: Ch 1, sc in first st, ch 2, [sc in next sc, ch 2] around, join. *(8 ch-2 sps)*

Rnd 3: (Sc, 3 dc, sc) in each ch-2 sp around, **do not join**. *(8 petals)*

Rnd 4: Working behind petals of last rnd, sc in beg sc of rnd 2, ch 3, [sc in next unworked sc of rnd 2, ch 3] around, join. *(8 ch-3 sps)*

Rnd 5: (Sc, 5 dc, sc) in each ch-3 sp around, **do not join**. *(8 petals)*

Rnd 6: Working behind petals of last rnd, sc in beg sc of rnd 4, ch 4, [sc in next unworked sc of rnd 4, ch 4] around. *(8 ch-4 sps)*

Rnd 7: Sl st in each of first 2 chs of first ch-4, ch 1, sc in same ch-4 sp, ch 5, [sc in next ch-4 sp, ch 5] around, join. *(8 ch-5 sps)*

Rnd 8: Sl st in each of first 3 chs of first ch-5, **beg shell** *(see Special Stitches)* in same ch as last sl st, *ch 2, **V-st** *(see Special Stitches)* in center ch of next ch-5, ch 2**, **shell** *(see Special Stitch)* in center ch of next ch-5, rep from * around, ending last rep at **, join with sl st in third ch of beg ch-3. *(4 shells; 4 V-sts)*

Rnd 9: Sl st in each of next 2 dc and in ch sp of next shell, (beg shell, ch 2, 3 dc) in same ch sp, *ch 2, 7 dc in ch sp of next V-st, ch 2**, (shell, ch 2, 3 dc) in ch sp of next shell, rep from * around, ending last rep at **, join

Rnd 10: Sl st in each of next 2 dc and in next ch-2 sp, beg shell in same ch sp, *ch 5, shell in next ch-2 sp, ch 2, sk next ch-2 sp, dc in next dc, [ch 1, dc in next dc] 6 times, ch 2, sk next ch-2 sp**, shell in next ch-2 sp, rep from * around, ending last rep at **, join.

Rnd 11: Sl st in each of next 2 dc and in ch sp of next shell, beg shell in same ch sp, *ch 2, V-st in center ch of next ch-5, ch 2, shell in next shell, ch 2, sc in next ch-1 sp, [ch 3, sc in next ch-1 sp] 5 times, ch 2**, shell in next shell, rep from * around, ending last rep at **, join.

Rnd 12: Sl st in each of next 2 dc and in ch sp of next shell, beg shell in same ch sp, *ch 2, dc in next V-st,(**picot**—*see Special Stitches*, dc) 4 times in same ch sp, ch 2, shell in next shell, ch 2, [**cl** *(see Special Stitches)* in next ch-3 sp, ch 2] 5 times**, shell in next shell, rep from * around, ending last rep at **, join.

Rnd 13: Sl st in each of next 2 dc and in ch sp of next shell, beg shell in same ch sp, *ch 2, sk next ch-2 sp, dc in next dc, [ch 1, picot, ch 1, dc in next dc] 4 times, ch 2, shell in next shell, ch 2, sk next ch-2 sp, sc in next ch-2 sp, [ch 3, sc in next ch-2 sp] 3 times, ch 2**, shell in next shell, rep from * around, ending last rep at **, join.

Rnd 14: Sl st in each of next 2 dc and in ch sp of next shell, beg shell in same ch sp, *ch 2, sk next ch-2 sp, dc in next dc, [ch 2, picot, ch 2, dc in next dc] 4 times, ch 2, shell in next shell, ch 2, [cl in next ch-3 sp, ch 2] 3 times**, shell in next shell, rep from * around, ending last rep at **, join.

Rnd 15: Sl st in each of next 2 dc and in ch sp of next shell, beg shell in same ch sp, *ch 2, sk next ch-2 sp, [dc in next dc, ch 3, picot, ch 3] twice, tr in next dc, [ch 3, picot, ch 3, dc in next dc] twice, ch 2, shell in next shell, ch 2, sk next ch-2 sp, sc in next ch-2 sp, ch 3, sc in next ch-2 sp, ch 2**, shell in next shell, rep from * around, ending last rep at **, join.

Rnd 16: Sl st in each of next 2 dc and in ch sp of next shell, beg shell in same ch sp, *ch 2, sk next ch-2 sp, dc in next dc, ch 4, picot, ch 4, dc in next dc, ch 4, picot, ch 4, tr in next tr, [ch 4, picot, ch 4, dc in next dc] twice, ch 2, shell in next shell, ch 2, cl in next ch-3 sp, ch 2**, shell in next shell, rep from * around, ending last rep at **, join.

Rnd 17: Sl st in each of next 2 dc and in ch sp of next shell, beg shell in same ch sp, *ch 4, dc in next ch sp, [ch 4, dc in next ch sp, ch 4, sk next picot, dc in next ch sp] twice, ch 3, (tr, ch 3) twice in next tr, dc in next ch sp, [ch 4, sk next picot, dc in next ch sp, ch 4, dc in next ch sp] twice, ch 4**, shell in next shell, (3 dc, ch 1) in next shell, **turn,** sl st in ch-2 sp of last shell made, ch 1, **turn,** 3 dc in same ch sp as last 3 dc made, rep from * around, ending last rep at **, (3 dc, ch 1) in last shell, sl st in ch-2 sp of beg shell, ch 1, 3 dc in same shell as last 3 dc made, join. Fasten off.

Rnd 18: With RS facing, join thread and blending filament with sl st in any corner ch-3 sp, ch 1, beg shell in same ch sp, *5 sc in corner ch-3 sp, sc in next tr, [3 sc in next ch sp, sc in next dc] 6 times, sc in each of next 2 dc, sc in next ch sp, sc in sl st joining 2 shells, sc in next ch sp, sc in each of next 3 dc, [3 sc in next sp, sc in next dc] 5 times, 3 sc in next ch sp, sc in next tr, rep from * around, join with sl st in beg sc. Fasten off.

Block each Side to 7¼ inches square; let dry.

With sewing needle and sewing thread, using photo as a guide, sew one ⅛-inch pearl at center of each flower on each Side. Sew one ⅛-inch pearl over each ch-2 sp on rnd 2 of each flower on each Side. Sew one ⅛-inch pearl at base of each cl on each pineapple of each Side. Sew one 3⁄16-inch pearl at base of each pair of corner tr on rnd 17 on each Side.

JOINING SIDES
With WS tog, working through both thicknesses, join thread and blending filament with sl st in first sc to the left of any corner sc on rnd 18, ch 1, sc in same st, *[sk next 2 sts, shell in next st, sk next 2 sts, sc in next st] 10 times**, 2 sc in corner sc, sc in next st, rep from * around, ending last rep at ** *(3 sides joined)*. Fasten off.

TOP OPENING BORDER
With RS facing, join thread and blending filament with sl st in corner sc at right-hand side of top opening, ch 1, sc in same sc, *sc in next sc, [sk next 2 sts, shell in next st, sk next 2 sts, sc in next st] 10 times, sc in corner sc*, sc in corner st on next Side, rep between *, join with sl st in beg sc. Fasten off.

ZIPPER
Follow instructions on zipper package for shortening zipper. Sew zipper to WS of Top Opening Border.

LINING
Cut two pieces of fabric each 8½ x 15¾ inches for lining. With RS tog, allowing ⅝ inch for seam on each edge, sew pieces tog around all four sides to within 2 inches of beg.

Turn lining RS out; sew rem opening closed. Fold lining in half so two short edges come tog to form top opening. Sew side openings tog with invisible st.

Insert lining in purse. Sew top opening of lining to zipper.

ZIPPER PULL
Row 1 (RS): With size 10 hook, and size 30 thread and one strand blending filament held tog, ch 10, sl st in first ch to form ring, (beg shell, ch 2, shell) in ring, turn.

Row 2: Ch 3, shell in first ch-2 sp, ch 2, V-st in next ch-2 sp, ch 2, shell in last ch-2 sp, turn.

Row 3: Ch 3, shell in first shell, ch 2, 7 dc in V-st, ch 2, shell in last shell, turn.

Row 4: Ch 3, shell in first shell, ch 2, sk next ch-2 sp, dc in next dc, [ch 1, dc in next dc] 6 times, ch 2, shell in last shell, turn.

Row 5: Ch 3, shell in first shell, ch 2, sc in next ch-1 sp, [ch 3, sc in next ch-1 sp] 5 times, ch 2, shell in last shell sp, turn.

Row 6: Ch 3, shell in first shell, ch 2, [cl in next ch-3 sp, ch 2] 5 times, shell in last shell, turn.

Row 7: Ch 3, shell in first shell, ch 2, sk next ch-2 sp, sc in next ch-2 sp, [ch 3, sc in next ch-2 sp] 3 times, ch 2, shell in last shell, turn.

Row 8: Ch 3, shell in first shell, ch 2, [cl in next ch-3 sp, ch 2] 3 times, shell in last shell, turn.

Row 9: Ch 3, shell in first shell, ch 2, sk next ch-2 sp, sc in next ch-2 sp, ch 3, sc in next ch-2 sp, ch 2, shell in last shell, turn.

Row 10: Ch 3, shell in first shell, ch 2, cl in next ch-3 sp, ch 2, shell in last shell, turn.

Row 11: Ch 3, shell in first shell, (3 dc, ch 1) in next shell, **turn,** sl st in last shell made, ch 1, **turn,** 3 dc in same shell as last 3 dc. Fasten off.

With sewing needle and sewing thread, sew one 1⁄16-inch pearl at the base of each cl.

With size 30 thread and size 10 hook, ch 16, slip beg end of ch through hole in zipper tab and ring on row 1 of zipper pull, join with sl st in beg ch to form ring. Fasten off.

With small paintbrush, apply commercial fabric stiffener to one side of Zipper Pull; let dry.

Apply commercial fabric stiffener to opposite side of Zipper Pull; let dry.

SHOULDER STRAP
Wind second ball of size 10 thread into three separate balls. With three strands crochet thread and one strand blending filament held tog, work **sc cord** *(see Special Stitches)* until strap measures 36 inches or desired length. Fasten off.

Join one end of strap to rnd 1 of Top Border Opening at left side; join opposite end of strap to rnd 1 of Top Border Opening at right side.

Heavenly Pineapple Angel

Design by Jo Ann Maxwell

SKILL LEVEL
■■■□ INTERMEDIATE

FINISHED SIZE
19½ inches tall to top of wings

MATERIALS
- J. & P. Coats South Maid crochet cotton size 10 (400 yds per ball):
    1 ball #42 cream
- Size 5/1.90mm steel crochet hook or size needed to obtain gauge
- Stringlets doll hair by All Cooped Up
- 2-inch white dove
- 10 pink 1-inch satin roses with leaves
- Ribbon:
    2 yds ½-inch-wide gold
    2⅔ yds ⅛ inch-wide green
    4⅓ yds ¼ inch-wide green
- Pearl beads:
    10 size 6mm
    1 yd strung
- Small amount gold gypsophila
- Powdered blusher
- Small piece of nylon stocking
- 20 x 30-inch piece poster board
- 12-inch-tall plastic foam cone
- Wide cellophane tape
- Large bowl
- 2-inch-diameter plastic foam ball
- 1½-inch-diameter plastic foam ball
- 1½-inch plastic foam egg
- Hot-glue gun
- Fabric stiffener
- Plastic wrap
- Small amount polyester fiberfill
- Plastic drinking straw
- Clear spray paint

GAUGE
34 hdc = 5 inches

SPECIAL STITCHES
Beginning shell (beg shell): (Ch 3—*counts as first dc*, dc, ch 2, 2 dc) in indicated ch sp.
Shell: (2 dc, ch 2, 2 dc) in indicated ch sp.
Beginning double shell (beg dbl shell): (Beg shell, ch 2, 2 dc) in indicated ch sp.
Double shell (dbl shell): (Shell, ch 2, 2 dc) in indicated ch sp.

INSTRUCTIONS
BODY
Rnd 1: Beg at top of head, ch 6, sl st in first ch form a ring, ch 3 *(counts as first dc throughout)*, 31 dc in ring, join with sl st in third ch of beg ch-3. *(32 dc)*

Rnds 2–10: Ch 2 (counts as first hdc throughout), hdc in each st around, join with sl st in second ch of beg ch-2 at end of last rnd, insert plastic foam ball, join with sl st in top of beg ch 2. (32 hdc)

Rnd 11: Ch 1, sc in first st, sk next st, [sc in next st, sk next st] around, join with sl st in beg sc. (16 sc)

Rnd 12: Ch 3, dc in same st, 2 dc in each st around, join. (32 dc)

Rnds 13–17: Ch 3, dc in each st around, join. (32 dc)

Rnd 18: Ch 1, sc in first st, [ch 4, sc in next dc] around, ending with ch 2, hdc in beg sc to form last ch-4 sp. (32 ch-4 sps)

Rnds 19–21: Ch 1, sc in sp just formed, [ch 4, sc in next ch sp] around, ending with ch 2, hdc in beg sc to form last sp.

Rnds 22–26: Ch 1, sc in ch sp just formed, [ch 5, sc in next ch sp] around, ending with ch 2, dc in beg sc to form last ch sp.

Rnds 27–30: Ch 1, sc in ch sp just formed, [ch 6, sc in next ch sp] around, ending with ch 3, dc in beg sc to form last ch sp.

Rnds 31–34: Ch 1, sc in ch sp just formed, [ch 7, sc in next ch sp] around, ending with ch 3, tr in beg sc to form last ch sp.

Rnd 35: Sl st in sp just formed, **beg shell** (see Special Stitches) in same sp, *ch 3, sc in next ch sp, ch 3**, **shell** (see Special Stitches) in next sp, rep from * around, ending last rep at **, join in third ch of beg ch-3. (16 shells)

Rnd 36: Sl st in next dc and in ch-2 sp, beg shell in same sp, *ch 3, (dc, ch 2) in each of first 2 dc of next shell, (dc, ch 2) 4 times in ch-2 sp of same shell, dc in next dc of same shell, ch 2, dc in last dc of same shell, ch 3**, shell in next shell, rep from * around, ending last rep at **, join. (8 shells)

Rnd 37: Sl st in next dc and in ch-2 sp, beg shell in same sp, *ch 3, sk next ch-3 sp, [sc in next dc, ch 3] 8 times**, shell in next shell, rep from * around, ending last rep at **, join.

Rnd 38: Sl st in next dc and in ch-2 sp, beg shell in same sp, *ch 3, sk next ch-3 sp, [sc in next ch-3 sp, ch 3] 7 times**, shell in next shell, rep from * around, ending last rep at **, join.

Rnd 39: Sl st in next dc and in ch-2 sp, beg dbl shell in same sp, *ch 3, sk next ch-3 sp, [sc in next ch-3 sp, ch 3] 6 times**, dbl shell in next shell, rep from * around, ending last rep at **, join.

Rnd 40: Sl st in next dc and in ch-2 sp, beg shell in same ch sp, shell in next ch-2 sp, *ch 3, sk next ch-3 sp, [sc in next ch-3 sp, ch 3] 5 times**, shell in each of next ch-2 sps, rep from * around, ending last rep at **, join. Fasten off.

FIRST PINEAPPLE

Row 41: Join thread with sl st in ch sp of first unworked shell on rnd 40 to the right of next pineapple, beg shell in same ch sp, ch 3, sk next ch-3 sp, [sc in next ch-3 sp, ch 3] 4 times, shell in next shell, turn.

Row 42: Ch 3, shell in first shell, ch 3, sk next ch-3 sp, [sc in next ch-3 sp, ch 3] 3 times, shell in next shell, turn.

Row 43: Ch 3, shell in ch sp of first shell, ch 3, sk next ch-3 sp, [sc in next ch-3 sp, ch 3] twice, shell in next shell, turn.

Row 44: Ch 3, shell in first shell, ch 3, sk next ch-3 sp, sc in next ch-3 sp, ch 3, shell in next shell, turn.

Row 45: Ch 3, shell in each of next 2 shells, ch 3, sl st in first dc of first shell of last row. Fasten off.

Next rows: Rep rows 41–45 for each of rem seven Pineapples.

WINGS
Make 2.

Row 1: Ch 4, sl st in first ch to form ring, ch 3 (counts as first dc), 6 dc in ring, turn. (7 dc)

Row 2: Ch 6 (counts as first dc, ch-3), dc in next dc, [ch 3, dc in next dc] 5 times, turn.

Row 3: Ch 7 (counts as first dc, ch-4), [dc in next dc, ch 4] 5 times, sk 3 chs, dc in next ch, turn.

Row 4: Beg shell in first dc, [shell in next dc] 5 times, sk next 4 chs, shell in next ch, turn. (7 shells)

Row 5: Ch 3, shell in first shell, [ch 1, shell in next shell] twice, ch 1, dc in ch sp of next shell, (ch 1, dc) 7 times in same ch sp, [ch 1, shell in next shell] 3 times, turn.

Row 6: Ch 3, shell in first shell, ch 1, dc in next shell, (ch 1, dc) 5 times in same ch sp, ch 1, shell in next shell, ch 3, sk next ch-1 sp, [sc in next dc, ch 3] 8 times, shell in next shell, ch 1, dc in next shell, (ch 1, dc) 9 times in same ch sp, ch 1, shell in next shell, turn.

Row 7: Ch 3, shell in first shell, ch 3, sk next ch-1 sp, [sc in next dc, ch 3] 10 times, shell in next shell, ch 3, sk next ch-3 sp, [sc in next ch-3 sp, ch 3] 7 times, shell in next shell, ch 3, sk next ch-1 sp, [sc in next dc, ch 3] 6 times, shell in next shell, turn.

Row 8: Ch 3, shell in first shell, ch 3, sk next ch-3 sp, [sc in next ch-3 sp, ch 3] 5 times, shell in next shell, ch 3, sk next ch-3 sp, [sc in next ch-3 sp, ch 3] 6 times, shell in next shell, ch 3, sk next ch-3 sp, [sc in next ch-3 sp, ch 3] 9 times, shell in next shell, turn.

Row 9: Ch 3, shell in first shell, ch 3, sk next ch-3 sp, [sc in next ch-3 sp, ch 3] 8 times, dbl shell in next shell, ch 3, sk next ch-3 sp, [sc in next ch-3 sp, ch 3] 5 times, dbl shell in next shell, ch 3, sk next ch-3 sp, [sc in next ch-3 sp, ch 3] 4 times, shell in next shell, turn.

BOTTOM PINEAPPLE

Rows 10–13: Rep Rows 42–45 of First Pineapple on Body.

CENTER PINEAPPLE

Row 10: Join with sl st in next unworked ch-2 sp of row 9, beg shell in same ch sp, ch 3, sk next ch-3 sp, [sc in next ch-3 sp, ch 3] 4 times, shell in next ch-2 sp, turn.

Rows 11–14: Rep rows 42–45 of First Pineapple on Body.

TOP PINEAPPLE

Row 10: Join with sl st in next unworked ch-2 sp of row 9, beg shell in same ch sp, ch 3, sk next ch-3 sp, [sc in next ch-3 sp, ch 3] 7 times, shell in next shell, turn.

Row 11: Ch 3, shell in first shell, ch 3, sk next ch-3 sp, [sc in next ch-3 sp, ch 3] 6 times, shell in next shell, turn.

Row 12: Ch 3, shell in first shell, ch 3, sk next ch-3 sp, [sc in next ch-3 sp, ch 3] 5 times, shell in next shell, turn.

Row 13: Ch 3, shell in first shell, ch 3, sk next ch-3 sp, [sc in next ch-3 sp, ch 3] 4 times, shell in next shell, turn.

Rows 14–17: Rep rows 42–45 of First Pineapple on Body.

SLEEVE
Make 2.

Rnd 1: Ch 4, sl st in first ch to form ring, ch 1, sc in ring, [ch 4, sc in ring] 7 times, ch 2, hdc in beg sc to form last ch-4 sp. *(8 ch-4 sps)*

Rnds 2–6: Ch 1, sc in sp just formed, [ch 4, sc in next ch sp] around, ending with ch 2, hdc in beg sc to form last sp. At end of last rnd, cover small piece of polyester fiberfill with plastic wrap, insert in sleeve. *(8 ch-4 sps)*

Rnd 7: Ch 1, beg in ch sp just formed, sc in each ch sp around, join with sl st in beg sc. *(8 sc)*

Rnds 8–13: Ch 3, dc in each st around, join sl st in third ch of beg ch-3. At end of last rnd, fasten off. *(8 dc)*

SHAPING

1. Cut poster board to make 12-inch-tall cone with 9-inch-diameter opening at bottom and 2-inch-diameter opening at top; tape tog with wide cellophane tape.
2. Place plastic foam cone inside paper cone, trimming as necessary to fit; tape to inverted bowl.
3. Cut 2-inch-diameter plastic foam ball in half; place flat side down on top of cone. Cover all with plastic wrap.
4. Apply fabric stiffener to Angel, squeeze out excess. Cover plastic foam egg with small piece of nylon stocking, then with plastic wrap; place in bodice, wide end first. Trim excess plastic wrap and pantyhose, leaving enough to grasp with pliers when removing egg later.
5. Place angel over cone, wrapping a thread tightly around rnd 11 of Body to shape neck, and less tightly between rnds 16 and 17 of Body to shape waist. Let dry.
6. Cut thread from waist only; remove egg with pliers, twisting fabric to pull out.
7. Apply fabric stiffener to Wings; pin tog to dry with piece of plastic wrap between so Wings will be same shape.
8. Cut drinking straw in half; place one piece in bottom of each Sleeve. Apply fabric stiffener to Sleeves; let dry.
9. Remove straws. Remove polyester fiberfill and plastic wrap with a crochet hook through ch-4 sps of upper sleeve.

FINISHING

1. Lightly spray all pieces with clear spray paint; let dry.
2. Wrap length of ¼-inch-wide ribbon twice around bodice, crossing at front as shown in photo; glue ends tog in back.
3. Bend Wings at center; glue to back of Angel with largest pineapple at top. Using photo as a guide, glue Sleeves to sides of Body.
4. Weave rem ¼-inch-wide green and gold ribbons through sps around bottom of skirt above pineapples. Decorate with gold gypsophila, seven roses and 6mm pearls, as shown in photo.
5. Cut doll hair approximately 5 inches long; glue to head; Loosely wrap small length of strung pearls twice across top of head for halo; glue to secure. Glue small sprig of gold gypsophila to hair.
6. Cut two 24-inch lengths of ⅛-inch-wide ribbon. Holding both tog, tie a bow; glue to outside of Sleeve at rnd 7, trimming ends as desired. Rep for opposite Sleeve.
7. Glue dove between bottoms of Sleeves, adding green ribbon, strings of pearls, gold gypsophila and three rem satin roses as shown in photo.
8. Lightly apply small amount of blusher.❑❑

Pineapple Sachet

Design by Florence Schliska

SKILL LEVEL
 INTERMEDIATE

FINISHED SIZE
4 x 4¾ inches

MATERIALS
- Crochet cotton size 10:
  85 yds white
  40 yds peach
- Size 7/1.65mm steel hook or size needed to obtain gauge
- Tapestry needle
- Sewing needle
- Sewing thread
- 6 x 12-inch piece white fabric
- 20 potpourri pearl beads
- 46 inches ⅜-inch-wide peach ribbon
- Fiberfill

GAUGE
5 dc = 1 inch

SPECIAL STITCH
Shell: (2 dc, ch 3, 2 dc) in indicated st.

INSTRUCTIONS

PINEAPPLE
Make 2.

Row 1: With white, ch 22, sc in 13th ch from hook *(lp made)*, ch 12, **shell** *(see Special Stitch)* in fourth ch from hook, ch 8, 11 dc in ch lp made, ch 8, shell in first ch of starting ch, turn.

Row 2: Ch 1, sk first dc, sl st in next dc, ch 3, shell in ch sp of shell, ch 8, dc in first dc of dc group, [ch 1, dc in next dc] 10 times, ch 8, shell in ch sp of shell, turn.

Row 3: Ch 3, shell in shell, ch 8, sc in next ch-1 sp, [ch 3, sc in next ch-1 sp] 9 times, ch 8, shell in shell, turn.

Row 4: Ch 3, shell in shell, ch 7, sc in next ch-3 sp, [ch 3, sc in next ch-3 sp] 8 times, ch 7, shell in shell, turn.

Row 5: Ch 3, shell in shell, ch 7, sc in next ch-3 sp, [ch 3, sc in next ch-3 sp] 7 times, ch 7, shell in shell, turn.

Row 6: Ch 3, shell in shell, ch 6, sc in next ch-3 sp, [ch 3, sc in next ch-3 sp] 6 times, ch 6, shell in shell, turn.

Row 7: Ch 3, shell in shell, ch 6, sc in next ch-3 sp, [ch 3, sc in next ch-3 sp] 5 times, ch 6, shell in shell, turn.

Row 8: Ch 3, shell in shell, ch 5, sc in next ch-3 sp, [ch 3, sc in next ch-3 sp] 4 times, ch 5, shell in shell, turn.

Row 9: Ch 3, shell in shell, ch 5, sc in next ch-3 sp, [ch 3, sc in next ch-3 sp] 3 times, ch 5, shell in shell, turn.

Row 10: Ch 3, shell in shell, ch 4, sc in next ch-3 sp, [ch 3, sc in next ch-3 sp] twice, ch 4, shell in shell, turn.

Row 11: Ch 3, shell in shell, ch 4, sc in next ch-3 sp, ch 3, sc in next ch-3 sp, ch 4, shell in shell, turn

Row 12: Ch 3, shell in shell, ch 4, sc in next ch-3 sp, ch 4, shell in shell, turn.

Row 13: Ch 3, shell in each of first 2 shells, ch 3, sl st in same ch-3 sp of last shell. Fasten off.

Center Trim
With RS facing, join peach with sl st in base of ch sp at the bottom of the 11th dc of row 1, ch 1, sc in same ch sp, ch 4, sc in end of dc of pineapple, (3 dc, ch 3, 3 dc) in end of next row, [ch 1, sc in end of next row, ch 1, (3 dc, ch 3, 3 dc) in end of next row] 4 times, (sc, hdc, dc) in end of row 11, ch 3, (dc, hdc, sc) in opposite end of row 11, [(3 dc, ch 3, 3 dc) in end of next row, ch 1, sc in end of next row] 4 times, (3 dc, ch 3, 3 dc) in end of row 2, ch 1, sc in end of row 1, ch 4, join with sl st in beg sc. Fasten off.

With peach, rep Center Trim on second Pineapple in same manner, **do not fasten off** *(this section is front)*.

JOINING SECTIONS

Working in second section only, ch 3 *(counts as first dc)*, (2 dc, ch 3, 3 dc) in same st, ch 8, (3 dc, ch 3, 3 dc) in end of dc of shell of row 1, sc in ch-3 with WS of both sections tog, matching stitches and working through both thicknesses, (3 dc, ch 3, 3 dc) in same ch 3 as last sc, [ch 2, sc in next ch-3 sp of shell, ch 2, (3 dc, ch 3, 3 dc) in next ch-3 sp] 6 times, sc in next ch-3 sp, ch 2, (3 dc, ch 3, 3 dc) in each of next 2 shell, ch 2, sc in next ch-3 sp, (3 dc, ch 3, 3 dc) in same ch sp as last sc, [ch 2, sc in next ch-3 sp, ch 2, (3 dc, ch 3, 3 dc) in next ch-3 sp] 5 times, working in second section only, sc in next ch-3 sp, (3 dc, ch 3, 3 dc) in edge of dc shell, ch 8, join with sl st in top of beg ch-3. Fasten off. *(1 shell at center bottom of pineapple, 7 shells up side edge, 2 shell at center top of pineapple, 7 shells down opposite side of pineapple)*

PILLOW INSERT

1. Following heart illustration, cut 2 pieces from fabric. Leaving the top of heart open, sew heart closed according to illustration.
2. Turn RS out. Stuff firmly with fiberfill and potpourri pearls. With sewing needle and thread, sew opening closed.
3. Insert fabric heart into crocheted piece. With sewing needle and thread, tack ch-3 of first Joining Section shell to opposite side of starting ch of first section. Tack shells at each side of center bottom shell to first section.
4. Cut a length of ribbon 22 inches in length. Cut remainder of ribbon in half, 12 inches each length.
5. Working the 22-inch length, fold piece in half, start at the center top point of pineapple, *(ch-4 sps of row 12)*. Using ribbon illustration as a guideline, weave ribbon WS up under chains on each side of opening, pull up between opening to form a lp, turn lp RS out while turning the whole ribbon, pull both ends until a point in the ribbon forms. Continue weaving the ribbon over and under each chain, making a point whenever the ribbon is over the chain, until all but one chain is used on each side. Weave ends through chain lp at the center, tie ends of ribbon a bow, trim ends even.
6. Weave 12-inch length of ribbon through ch sp on opposite side at base of Pineapple and tie ends in a bow, trim ends even.
7. For **hanging lp,** weave rem length of ribbon under beg shell of Joining Sections, tie end in a knot about 1 inch from ends. ❑❑

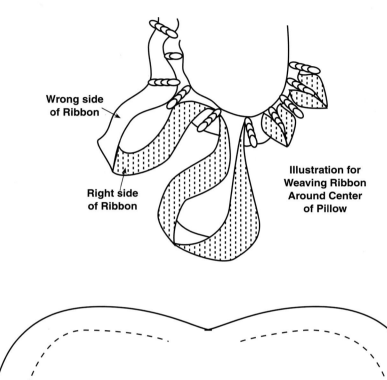

Illustration for Weaving Ribbon Around Center of Pillow

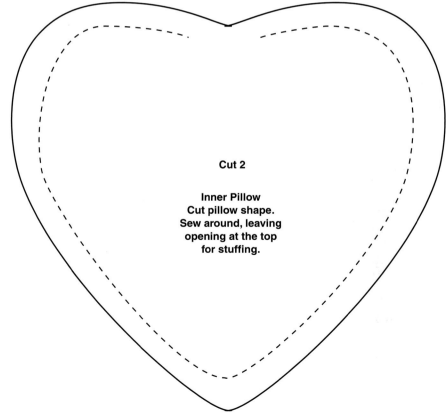

Cut 2

Inner Pillow
Cut pillow shape.
Sew around, leaving opening at the top for stuffing.

Antique Pineapples Valance

Design by Addie May Bodwell

SKILL LEVEL
■■■□ INTERMEDIATE

FINISHED SIZE
39 inches across

MATERIALS
- Crochet cotton size 10: 260 yds white
- Size 8/1.50mm steel crochet hook or size needed to obtain gauge

GAUGE
9 sts = 1 inch; dtr = 5/8 inches tall

PATTERN NOTES
After row 2, fasten off at end of each row. All rows are worked on right side.

A roll stitch may be substituted for a double treble crochet and chain-1.

INSTRUCTIONS
VALANCE
Row 1 (RS): Ch 338, dc in fourth ch from hook *(first 3 chs count as first dc)* and in each ch across, turn. *(336 dc)*

Row 2: Ch 1, sc in first st, [ch 7, sk next 4 sts, sc in next st] across, turn. *(67 ch sps)*

Row 3 (RS): Ch 5, (tr, ch 6, tr) in first ch sp, [ch 5, tr in next ch sp, ch 5, dc in next ch sp, ch 5, (tr, ch 6, tr) in next ch sp] across, ch 5, sl st in last sc, **do not turn.** Fasten off *(see Pattern Notes)*.

Row 4: Join in first ch-6 sp, ch 5, for **pineapple,** (dtr, ch 1) 8 times in same sp, [ch 6, (dtr, ch 1) 4 times in next ch-6 sp, ch 6, for **pineapple,** (dtr, ch 1) 8 times in next ch-6 sp] across, dtr in top of last ch-5.

Row 5: Join with sc between first 2 dtr of first pineapple, [ch 5, sc between next 2 dtr] 6 times, *ch 7, (dtr, ch 1) 4 times in ch sp between second and third dtr of next 4-dtr group, ch 6, sc between first 2 dtr of next pineapple, [ch 5, sc between next 2 dtr] 6 times, rep from * across.

Row 6: Join with sc in first ch sp of first pineapple, ch 5, sc in next ch sp] 5 times, *ch 7, (dtr, ch 1) 4 times in ch sp between second and third dtr of next 4 dtr-group, ch 6, sc in first ch sp of next pineapple, [ch 5, sc in next ch sp] 5 times, rep from * across.

Row 7: Join with sc in first ch sp of first pineapple, [ch 5, sc in next ch sp] 4 times, *ch 7, (dtr, ch 1) 6 times in ch sp between second and third dtr of next 4-dtr group, ch 6, sc in first ch sp of next pineapple, [ch 5, sc in next ch sp] 4 times, rep from * across.

Row 8: Join with sc in first ch sp of first pineapple, [ch 5, sc in next ch sp] 3 times, *ch 7, (dtr, ch 1) 4 times in ch sp between second and third dtr of next 6-dtr group, ch 6, (dtr, ch 1) 4 times between fourth and fifth dtr of same 6-dtr group, ch 6, sc in first ch sp of next pineapple, [ch 5, sc in next ch sp] 3 times, rep from * across.

Row 9: Join with sc in first ch sp of first pineapple, [ch 5, sc in next ch sp] twice, *ch 7, (dtr, ch 1) 4 times in ch sp between second and third dtr of next 4-dtr group, ch 4, (tr, ch 6, tr) in next ch-7 sp, ch 5, (dtr, ch 1) 4 times in ch sp between second and third dtr of next 4-dtr group, ch 6, sc in first ch sp of next pineapple, [ch 5, sc in next ch sp] twice, rep from * across.

Row 10: Join with sc in first ch sp of first pineapple, ch 5, sc in next ch sp, *ch 7, (dtr, ch 1) 4 times in ch sp between second and third dtr of next 4-dtr group, ch 5, (dtr, ch 1) 8 times in ch-6 sp between next 2 tr, ch 5, (dtr, ch 1) 4 times in ch sp between second and third dtr of next 4-dtr group, ch 6, sc in first ch sp of next pineapple, ch 5, sc in next ch sp, rep from * across.

Row 11: For **edging,** with RS facing you, beg at outer edge of first pineapple, join with sc in beg ch at bottom of first dc, ch 7, sc in first ch sp of row 2, ch 7, sc in ch-5 sp at beg of row 4, ch 7, sc in first ch sp of row 5, ch 7, sc in first ch sp of row 8, ch 7, sc in center of ch sp at point of pineapple, *ch 7, sc in center of next ch-7 sp, ch 7, sc in ch sp between second and third dtr of next 4-dtr group, ch 7, sc in next ch-5 sp, [ch 7, sk next 2 dtr, sc in next ch sp between dtr] 3 times, ch 7 sc in next ch-5 sp, ch 7, sc in ch sp between second and third dtr of next 4-dtr group, ch 7, sc in center of next ch-7 sp, ch 7, sc in center of next ch sp at point of next pineappple, rep from * across to last pineapple, work down side of last pineapple in same manner as first pineapple, ending with sc in beg ch at bottom of last dc.

Row 12: Join with sc in first ch-7 sp of row 11, (4 sc, ch 3, 5 sc) in same ch sp, (5 sc, ch 3, 5 sc) in each ch-7 sp across. Fasten off.

Ribbons & Lace Fan

Design by Mrs. N. J. Richardson

SKILL LEVEL
INTERMEDIATE

FINISHED SIZE
10 inches tall

MATERIALS
- Crochet cotton size 20: 220 yds white
- Size 13/0.85mm steel crochet hook or size needed to obtain gauge
- Ribbon:
  - 2/3 yd 1-inch-wide box pleated *(optional)*
  - 3/4 yd 1/4-inch-wide *(optional)*
- 9-inch folding fan

GAUGE
11 sts = 1 inch, tr = 1/4 inch high

SPECIAL STITCHES
Shell: (2 dc, ch 2, 2 dc) in indicated st or ch sp.
Shell increase (shell inc): (2 dc, ch 2, 2 dc, ch 2, 2 dc) in indicated st of ch sp.

INSTRUCTIONS
LACE
Row 1: Ch 104, **shell** *(see Special Stitches)* in fourth ch from hook, *sk next 4 chs, (dc, ch 2, dc) in next ch, sk next 4 chs, shell in next ch, rep from * across, turn. (11 shells)
Row 2: Ch 3, shell in ch sp of first shell, [6 tr in next ch sp, shell in next shell] across, turn.
Row 3: Ch 3, shell in first shell, *sk next tr, [ch 4, sl st in next sp between tr] 5 times, ch 4, shell in next shell, rep from * across, turn.
Row 4: Ch 3, **shell inc** *(see Special Stitches)* in first shell, *sk next ch sp, [ch 4, sl st in next ch sp] 4 times, ch 4, shell inc in next shell, rep from * across, turn.
Row 5: Ch 3, shell in each ch sp of first shell inc, *sk next ch sp, [ch 4, sl st in next ch sp] 3 times, ch 4, shell in each ch sp of next shell inc, rep from * across, turn.
Row 6: Ch 3, shell in first shell, (dc, ch 2, dc) in next sp between shells, shell in next shell, *sk next ch sp, [ch 4, sl st in next ch sp] twice, ch 4, shell in next shell, (dc, ch 2, dc) in next sp between shells, shell in next shell, rep from * across, turn.
Row 7: Ch 3, shell in first shell, 8 tr in next ch-2 sp, shell in next shell, *sk next ch sp, dc in next ch sp, shell in next shell, 8 tr in next ch sp, shell in next shell, rep from * across, turn.
Row 8: Ch 3, shell in first shell, sk next 2 dc, and next tr, [ch 4, sl st in next sp between tr] 7 times, ch 4, *2 dc in next shell, ch 2, 2 dc in next dc, ch 2, 2 dc in next shell, sk next 2 dc and next tr, [ch 4, sl st in next sp between tr] 7 times, ch 4, rep from * across, ending with shell in last shell, turn.
Row 9: Ch 3, shell in first shell, sk next ch sp, [ch 4, sl st in next ch sp] 6 times, ch 4, *sk next ch sp, 2 dc in next ch sp, ch 2, 2 dc in next ch sp, sk next ch sp, [ch 4, sl st in next ch sp] 6 times, ch 4, rep from * across, ending with shell in last shell, turn.
Row 10: Ch 3, shell in first shell, sk next ch sp, [ch 4, sl st in next ch sp] 5 times, ch 4, *sk next ch sp, shell in next ch sp, sk next ch sp, [ch 4, sl st in next ch sp] 5 times, ch 4, rep from * across, ending with shell in last shell, turn.

Row 11: Ch 3, shell inc in first shell, *sk next ch sp, [ch 4, sl st in next ch sp] 4 times, ch 4, shell inc in next shell, rep from * across, turn.

Row 12: Ch 3, shell in each ch sp of first shell inc, *sk next ch sp, [ch 4 sl st in next ch sp] 3 times, ch 4, sk next ch sp, shell in each ch sp of next shell inc, rep from * across, turn.

Row 13: Ch 3, shell in first shell, (dc, ch 2, dc) in next sp between shells, shell in next shell, *sk next ch sp, [ch 4, sl st in next ch sp] twice, ch 4, shell in next shell, (dc, ch 2, dc) in next sp between shells, shell in next shell, rep from * across, turn.

Row 14: Ch 3, shell in first shell, 10 tr in next ch sp, *shell in next shell, sk next ch sp, dc in next ch sp, sk next ch sp, shell in next shell, 10 tr in next ch sp, rep from * across, ending with shell in last shell, turn.

Row 15: Ch 3, shell in first shell, sk next 2 dc and next tr, [ch 4, sl st in next sp between tr] 9 times, ch 4, *2 dc in next ch sp, ch 2, 2 dc in next dc, ch 2, 2 dc in next ch sp, sk next 2 dc and next tr, [ch 4, sl st in next sp between tr] 9 times, ch 4, rep from * across, ending with shell in last shell, turn.

Row 16: Ch 3, shell in first shell, sk next ch sp, [ch 4, sl st in next ch sp] 8 times, ch 4, *sk next ch sp, 2 dc in next ch sp, ch 2, 2 dc in next ch sp, sk next ch sp, [ch 4, sl st in next ch sp] 8 times, ch 4, rep from * across, ending with shell in last shell, turn.

Row 17: Ch 3, shell in first shell, sk next ch sp, [ch 4, sl st in next ch sp] 7 times, ch 4, sk next ch sp, *shell in next ch sp, sk next ch sp, [ch 4, sl st in next ch sp] 7 times, ch 4, sk next ch sp, rep from * across, ending with shell in last shell, turn.

Row 18: Ch 3, shell inc in first shell, *sk next ch sp, [ch 4, sl st in next ch sp] 6 times, ch 4, sk next ch sp, shell inc in next shell, rep from * across, turn.

Row 19: Ch 3, shell in each ch sp of first shell inc, *sk next ch sp, [ch 4, sl st in next ch sp] 5 times, ch 4, shell in each ch sp of next shell inc, rep form * across, turn.

Row 20: Ch 3, shell in first shell, (dc, ch 2, dc) in next sp between shells, shell in next shell, *sk next ch sp, [ch 4, sl st in next ch sp] 4 times, ch 4, shell in next shell, (dc, ch 2, dc) in next sp between shells, shell in next shell, rep from * across, turn.

Row 21: Ch 3, shell in first shell, ch 2, (dc, ch 2, dc) in next ch sp, ch 2, *shell in next shell, sk next ch sp, [ch 4, sl st in next ch sp] 3 times, ch 4, shell in next shell, ch 2, (dc, ch 2, dc) in next ch sp, ch 3, rep from * across, ending with shell in last shell, turn.

Row 22: Ch 3, shell in first shell, ch 2, (dc, ch 2, dc) in next ch sp, ch 2, dc in next ch sp, ch 2, (dc, ch 2, dc) in next ch sp, ch 2, shell in next shell, *sk next ch sp, [ch 4, sl st in next ch sp] twice, ch 4, shell in next shell, ch 2, (dc, ch 2, dc) in next ch sp, ch 2, (dc, ch 2, dc) in next ch sp, ch 2, shell in next shell, rep from * across, turn.

Row 23: Ch 3, shell in first shell, ch 2, (dc, ch 2, dc) in next ch sp, [ch 2, dc in next ch sp] 4 times, ch 2, (dc, ch 2, dc) in next ch sp, ch 2, shell in next shell, *sk next ch sp, dc in next ch sp, shell in next shell, ch 2, (dc, ch 2, dc) in next ch sp, [ch 2, dc in next ch sp] 4 times, ch 2, (dc, ch 2, dc) in next ch sp, ch 2, shell in next shell, rep from * across, turn.

Row 24: [Ch 4, sl st in next ch sp] across. Fasten off.

FINISHING

Stretch Lace over slats on fan, glue or tack to slats with top edge extending 1 inch above top of slats.

Decorate with ribbon as desired.❏❏

Tabletop Treasure

SKILL LEVEL
INTERMEDIATE

FINISHED SIZE
14 x 21 inches

MATERIALS
- Crochet cotton size 10:
  800 yds pink
- Size 7/1.65mm steel crochet hook or size needed to obtain gauge

SPECIAL STITCHES
2-double crochet cluster (2-dc cl): Yo, insert hook in next ch sp, yo, pull lp through, yo, pull through 2 lps on hook, yo, insert hook in same ch sp, yo, pull lp through, yo, pull through 2 lps on hook, yo, pull through all lps on hook.
3-double crochet cluster (3-dc cl): Yo, insert hook in next ch sp, yo, pull lp through, yo, pull through 2 lps on hook, [yo, insert hook in same ch sp, yo, pull lp through, yo, pull through 2 lps on hook] twice, yo, pull through all lps on hook.
Shell: (3-dc cl, ch 3, 3-dc cl) in next ch sp.
Beginning shell (beg shell): (Sl st, ch 3—*counts as first dc*, 2-dc cl, ch 3, 3-dc cl) in first ch sp.

INSTRUCTIONS
CENTER MOTIF
Rnd 1: Ch 8, sl st in beg ch to form ring, ch 1, 12 sc in ring, join with sl st in beg sc. *(12 sc)*
Rnd 2: Ch 5 *(counts as first dc and ch-2 sp)*, [dc in next st, ch 2] around, join with sl st in third ch of beg ch-5. *(12 dc, 12 ch sps)*
Rnd 3: (Sl st, ch 3, **2-dc cl**—*see Special Stitches*) in first ch sp, ch 5, [**3-dc cl** *(see Special Stitches)* in next ch sp, ch 5] around, join with sl st in top of beg cl. *(12 cls, 12 ch sps)*
Rnd 4: [Ch 5, 3-dc cl in next ch-sp, ch 5, sl st next dc cl] around, join in with sl st in first ch of beg ch-5.
Rnd 5: Sl st in next ch, ch 1, sc in same ch sp, [ch 5, sc in next ch-5 sp] around, join with ch 2, dc in beg sc.
Rnd 6: Ch 1, sc around joining dc, ch 5, [sc in next ch sp, ch 5] around, join in beg sc.

First Pineapple
Row 1: Beg shell *(see Special Stitches)*, ch 2, (dc, ch 7, dc) in next ch sp, ch 2, **shell,** *(see Special Stitches)* in next ch sp, leaving rem sts unworked, turn.
Row 2: Ch 5, shell in ch sp of first shell, ch 2, 12 tr in next ch-7 sp, ch 2, shell in ch sp of next shell, dtr in top of last cl on previous row, turn.
Row 3: Ch 1, sl st in next cl, beg shell, ch 2, tr in next tr, [ch 1, tr in next tr] 11 times, ch 2, shell in last shell, turn.
Row 4: Ch 5, shell in ch sp of first shell, ch 4, sc in next ch-1 sp, [ch 3, sc in next ch-1 sp] 10 times, ch 4, shell in last shell, dtr in top of last cl on previous row, turn.
Row 5: Ch 1, sl st in next cl, beg shell, ch 4, sk next ch-4 sp, sc in next ch-3 sp, [ch 3, sc in next ch-3 sp] 9 times, ch 4, shell in last shell, turn.
Row 6: Ch 5, shell in first shell, ch 4, sk next ch-4 sp, sc in next ch-3 sp, [ch 3, sc in next ch-3 sp] 8 times, ch 4, shell in last shell, dtr in top of last cl on previous row, turn.
Row 7: Ch 1, sl st in next cl, beg shell, ch 4, sk next ch-4 sp, sc in next ch-3 sp, [ch 3, sc in next ch-3 sp] 7 times, ch 4, shell in last shell, turn.
Row 8: Ch 5, shell in first shell, ch 4, sk next ch-4 sp, sc in next ch-3 sp, [ch 3, sc in next ch-3 sp] 6 times, ch 4, shell in last shell, dtr in top of last cl on previous row, turn.

Row 9: Sl st in next cl, beg shell, ch 4, sk next ch-4 sp, sc in next ch-3 sp, [ch 3, sc in next ch-3 sp] 5 times, ch 4, shell in next shell, turn.

Row 10: Ch 5, shell in first shell, ch 4, sk next ch-4 sp, sc in next ch-3 sp, [ch 3, sc in next ch-3 sp] 4 times, ch 4, shell in last shell, tr in top of last cl on previous row, turn.

Row 11: Ch 1, sl st in next cl, beg shell, ch 4, sk next ch-4 sp, sc in next ch-3 sp, [ch 3, sc in next ch-3 sp] 3 times, ch 4, shell in last shell, turn.

Row 12: Ch 5, shell in first shell, ch 4, sk next ch-4 sp, sc in next ch-3 sp, [ch 3, sc in next ch-3 sp] twice, ch 4, shell in last shell, dtr in top of last cl on previous row, turn.

Row 13: Ch 1, sl st in next cl, beg shell, ch 4, sk next ch-4 sp, sc in next ch-3 sp, ch 3, sc in next ch-3 sp, ch 4, shell in last shell, turn.

Row 14: Ch 5, shell in first shell, ch 4, sk next ch-4 sp, sc in next ch-3 sp, ch 4, shell in last shell, dtr in top of last cl on previous row, turn.

Row 15: Ch 1, sl st in next cl, beg shell, ch 3, shell in last shell. Fasten off.

Second Pineapple
Sk next 9 ch sps of Center Motif, join in next ch sp, rep rows 1–15 of First Pineapple, turn, **do not fasten off.**

BORDER
Rnd 1: Beg shell, ch 11, **turn**, working along side of Pineapple, dc in next ch sp, [ch 8, dc in next ch sp] 5 times, *ch 8, yo twice, insert hook in next ch sp of same Pineapple, yo, pull lp through, [yo, pull through 2 lps on hook] twice, yo twice, sk next unworked ch sp of Center Motif, insert hook in next ch sp, yo, pull lp through, [yo, pull through 2 lps on hook] 4 times, ch 8, sk next ch sp, dc in next ch sp, ch 8, sc in next ch sp, ch 8, dc in next ch sp, ch 8, sk next ch sp, yo twice, insert hook in next ch sp, yo, pull lp through, [yo, pull through 2 lps on hook] twice, yo twice, insert hook in first ch sp of next Pineapple, yo, pull lp through, [yo, pull through 2 lps on hook] 4 times, [ch 8, dc in next ch sp of Pineapple] 6 times*, [ch 8, dc in next ch-3 sp of next shell at end of Pineapple] twice, working along opposite side of Pineapple, [ch 8, dc in next ch sp] 6 times, rep between * once, ch 8, join with sl st in third ch of beg ch-11.

Rnd 2: Sl st in each of next 4 chs, ch 3, dc in same ch sp, [ch 9, 2 dc in next ch sp] 5 times, ch 9, keeping last lp of each tr on hook, tr in each of next 2 ch sps, *(3 lps on hook)*, [yo, pull through 2 lps on hook] twice, [ch 9, 2 dc in next ch sp] twice, ch 9, keeping last lp of each tr on hook, tr in each of next 2 ch sps, [yo, pull through 2 lps on hook] twice, [ch 9, 2 dc in next ch sp] 7 times, ch 9, 2 dc in same ch sp, [ch 9, 2 dc in next ch sp] 6 times, ch 9, keeping last lp of each tr on hook, tr in each of next 2 ch sps, [yo, pull through 2 lps on hook] twice, [ch 9, 2 dc in next ch sp] twice, ch 9, keeping last lp of each tr on hook, tr in each of next 2 ch sps, [yo, pull through 2 lps on hook] twice, [ch 9, 2 dc in next ch sp] 7 times, ch 9, 2 dc in same sp, ch 9, join with sl st in third ch of beg ch-3.

Rnd 3: Sl st in next st, sl st in each of next 5 chs, (ch 8, dc) in same ch, [ch 4, (dc, ch 5, dc) in center ch of next ch-9] 14 times, [ch 4, (dc, ch 5, dc) in third ch of next ch-9, ch 4, sk 2 chs of same ch-9, (dc, ch 5, dc) in next ch, ch 4, (dc, ch 5, dc) in center ch of next ch-9] twice, [ch 4, (dc, ch 5, dc) in center ch of next ch-9] 14 times, *ch 4, (dc, ch 5, dc) in third ch of next ch-9, ch 4, sk next 2 chs of same ch-9, (dc, ch 5, dc) in next ch*, ch 4, (dc, ch 5, dc) in center ch of next ch-9, rep between * once, ch 4, join with sl st in third ch of beg ch-8. *(40 ch-5 sps, 40 ch-4 sps)*

Rnd 4: Beg shell, *ch 4, sk next ch-4 sp, 6 tr in next ch-5 sp, ch 4**, sk next ch-4 sp, shell in next ch-5 sp, rep from * around, ending last rep at **, join with sl st in top of beg cl.

Rnd 5: Beg shell, *ch 4, tr in next tr, [ch 1, tr in next tr] 5 times, ch 4**, shell in next shell, rep from * around, ending last rep at **, join.

Rnd 6: Beg shell, *ch 4, sk next ch-4 sp, sc in next ch-1 sp, [ch 3, sc in next ch-1 sp] 4 times, ch 4**, shell in next shell, rep from * around, ending last rep at **, join.

Rnd 7: Beg shell, *ch 4, sk next ch-4 sp, sc in next ch-3 sp, [ch 3, sc in next ch-3 sp] 3 times, ch 4**, shell in next shell, rep from * around ending last rep at **, join.

Rnd 8: Sl st in next ch sp, (ch 3, 2-dc cl) in same ch sp, [ch 3, 3-dc cl] twice in same ch sp, *ch 4, sk next ch-4 sp, sc in next ch-3 sp, [ch 3, sc in next ch-3 sp] twice, ch 4, 3-dc cl in next shell, [ch 3, 3-dc cl] twice in same shell, join.

Rnd 9: Beg shell, *ch 5, shell in next ch-3 sp, ch 4, sk next ch-4 sp, sc in next ch-3 sp, ch 3, sc in next ch-3 sp, ch 4, sk next ch-4 sp**, shell in next ch-3 sp, rep from * around, ending last rep at **, join.

Rnd 10: Beg shell, *ch 3, 6 tr in next ch-5 sp, ch 3, shell in next shell, ch 4, sk next ch-4 sp, sc in next ch-3 sp, ch 4**, shell in next shell, rep from * around, ending last rep at **, join.

Rnd 11: Beg shell, *ch 4, tr in next tr, [ch 1, tr in next tr] 5 times, ch 4, shell in next shell, ch 1**, shell in next shell, rep from * around, ending last rep at **, join.

Rnd 12: Beg shell, *ch 4, sk next ch-4 sp, sc in next ch-1 sp, [ch 3, sc in next ch-1 sp] 4 times, ch 4, shell in next shell, ch 3**, shell in next shell, rep from * around, ending last rep at **, join.

Rnd 13: Beg shell, *ch 4, sk next ch-4 sp, sc in next ch-3 sp, [ch 3, sc in next ch-3 sp] 3 times, ch 4, shell in next shell, ch 5**, shell in next shell, rep from * around, ending last rep at **, join.

Rnd 14: Beg shell, *ch 4, sk next

ch-4 sp, sc in next ch-3 sp, [ch 3, sc in next ch-3 sp] twice, ch 4, shell in next shell, ch 3, 5 dc in next ch-5 sp, ch 3**, shell in next shell, rep from * around, ending last rep at **, join.

Rnd 15: Beg shell, *ch 4, sk next ch-4 sp, sc in next ch-3 sp, ch 3, sc in next ch sp, ch 4, shell in next shell, ch 3, dc in next dc, [ch 1, dc in next dc] 4 times, ch 3**, shell in next shell, rep from * around, ending last rep at **, join.

Rnd 16: Beg shell, *ch 4, sk next ch-4 sp, sc in next ch-3 sp, ch 4, shell in next shell, ch 3, dc in next dc, [ch 2, dc in next dc] 4 times, ch 3**, shell in next shell, rep from * around, ending last rep at **, join.

Rnd 17: Beg shell, *ch 1, shell in next shell, ch 4, dc in next dc, [ch 4, dc in next dc] 4 times, ch 4**, shell in next shell, rep from * around, ending last rep at **, join.

Rnd 18: (Sl st, ch 3, 2-dc cl) in next ch sp, ch 1, 3-dc cl in next shell, (ch 5, dc) in each of next 2 dc, ch 5, (dc, ch 5, dc) in next dc, (ch 5, dc) in each of next 2 dc, ch 5, *[3-dc cl in next shell, ch 1, 3-dc cl in next shell, ch 5, (dc, ch 5) in each of next 5 dc] 5 times*, [3-dc cl in next shell, ch 1, 3-dc cl in next shell, (ch 5, dc) in each of next 2 dc, ch 5, (dc, ch 5, dc) in next dc, (ch 5, dc) in each of next 2 dc, ch 5] 5 times, rep between * once, [3-dc cl in next shell, ch 1, 3-dc cl in next shell, (ch 5, dc) in each of next 2 dc, ch 5, (dc, ch 5, dc) in next dc, (ch 5, dc) in each of next 2 dc, ch 5] 4 times, join.

Rnd 19: Ch 1, (sc, ch 4, sc) in next ch-1 sp, 4 sc next ch 5 sp, (3 sc, ch 4, 3 sc) in each of next 5 ch sps, 4 sc in next ch-5 sp, *[(sc, ch 4, sc) in next ch-1 sp, 4 sc in next ch-5 sp, (3 sc, ch 4, 3 sc) in each of next 4 ch sps, 4 sc in next ch-5 sp] 5 times, [(sc, ch 4, sc) in next ch-1 sp, 4 sc next ch-5 sp, (3 sc, ch 4, 3 sc) in each of next 5 ch sps, 4 sc in next ch-5 sp] 5 times, rep from * around, join with sl st in beg sc. Fasten off.

Oriental Jade

Design by Josie Rabier

SKILL LEVEL
INTERMEDIATE

FINISHED SIZE
20 inches in diameter

MATERIALS
- Crochet cotton size 10: 350 yds jade
- Size 7/1.65mm steel crochet hook or size needed to obtain gauge

GAUGE
Rnds 1–3 = 2 inches in diameter

SPECIAL STITCHES
Small V-stitch (small V-st): (Dc, ch 3, dc) in indicated st.
Large V-stitch (large V-st): (Dc, ch 5, dc) in indicated st.
Beginning shell (beg shell): Ch 3 *(counts as first dc)*, (2 dc, ch 2, 3 dc) in same st or ch sp as beg ch-3.
Shell: (3 dc, ch 2, 3 dc) in indicated st or ch sp.
Popcorn (pc): 7 dc in indicated st, drop lp from hook, insert hook in first dc of group, pick up dropped lp and pull through.

INSTRUCTIONS
DOILY

Rnd 1: Ch 8, sl st in first ch form ring, ch 1, 24 sc in ring, join with sl st in beg sc. *(24 sc)*

Rnd 2: Ch 3 *(counts as first dc throughout)*, dc in same st, 2 dc in each sc around, join with sl st in third ch of beg ch-3. *(48 dc)*

Rnd 3: Ch 3, dc in each dc around, join. *(48 dc)*

Rnd 4: Ch 7, [sk next 2 dc, sl st in next dc, ch 7] around, join with sl st in base of beg ch-7. *(16 ch-7 sps)*

Rnd 5: Sl st in ch-7 sp, ch 1, 7 sc in same sp, 7 sc in each ch sp around, join with sl st in beg sc. *(112 sc)*

Rnd 6: Sl st to fourth sc of 7-sc group, ch 6 *(counts as first dc and ch-3)*, dc in same st, ch 3, *sk next 2 sc, sl st in each of next 2 sc, ch 3, sk next 2 sc, **small V-st** (see Special Stitches) in next sc, ch 3, rep from * around, join with sl st in third ch of beg ch-6. *(16 small V-sts)*

Rnd 7: Sl st to ch-3 sp of small V-st, **beg shell** *(see Special Stitches)* in same ch sp, ch 3, *sk next 2 ch-3 sps, **shell** (see Special Stitches) in ch-3 sp of next V-st, ch 3, rep from * around, join with sl st in third ch of beg ch-3.

Rnd 8: Ch 3, *shell in ch-2 sp of next shell, sk next 2 dc of same shell, dc in next dc, ch 5**, dc in first dc of next shell, rep from * around, ending last rep at **, join. *(16 shells)*

Rnd 9: Ch 3, dc in each of next 3 dc, *3 dc in next ch-2 sp, dc in each of next 4 dc, sl st in next ch-5 sp, dc in each of next 4 dc, rep from * around, join. *(176 dc)*

Rnd 10: Sl st in third dc, ch 8 *(counts as first dc and ch-5)*, *sk next 2 dc, **large V-st** (see Special Stitches) in next dc, ch 5, sk next 2 dc, dc in next dc, sk next 4 dc, dc in next dc**, ch 5, rep from * around, ending last rep at **, join with sl st in third ch of beg ch-8.

Rnd 11: Sl st in each of next 3 chs of ch-5, *12 dc in ch-5 sp of next V-st, sl st in third ch of next ch-5 sp, ch 7, sl st in third ch of next ch-5 sp, rep from * around, join with sl st in first dc of 12-dc group. *(16 groups of 12 dc)*

Rnd 12: Ch 3, dc in each of next 11 dc, *ch 3, sl st in fourth ch of next ch-7 sp, ch 3**, dc in each of next 12 dc, rep from * around, ending last rep at **, join with sl st in third ch of beg ch-3.

Rnd 13: Ch 3, dc in each of next 11 dc, *3 dc in each of next 2 ch-3 sps, dc in each of next 12 dc, ch 3, dc in sl st between ch-3 sps, ch 3**, dc in each of next 12 dc, rep from * around, ending last rep at **, join. *(248 dc)*

Rnd 14: Ch 3, dc in each of next 29 dc, *ch 3, dc in dc between ch-3 sps, ch 3**, dc in each of next 30 dc, rep from * around, ending last rep at **, join.

Rnd 15: Ch 3, *sk next dc, dc in each of next 12 dc, sk next 2 dc, dc in each of next 12 dc, sk next dc, dc in next dc, ch 5, sk next ch-3 sp, sl st in next dc, ch 5, sk next ch-3 sp**, dc in next dc, rep from * around, ending last rep at **, join. *(8 groups of 26 dc)*

Rnd 16: Ch 3, *sk next dc, dc in each of next 10 dc, sk next 2 dc, dc in each of next 10 dc, sk next dc, dc in next dc, [ch 5, sl st in next ch-5 sp] twice, ch 5**, dc in next dc, rep from * around, ending last rep at **, join. *(8 groups of 22 dc)*

Rnd 17: Ch 3, *sk next dc, dc in each of next 8 dc, sk next 2 dc, dc in each of next 8 dc, sk next dc, dc in next dc, [ch 5, sl st in next ch-5 sp] 3 times, ch 5**, dc in next dc, rep from * around, ending last rep at **, join. *(8 groups of 18 dc)*

Rnd 18: Ch 3, *sk next dc, dc in each of next 6 dc, sk next dc, dc in each of next 6 dc, sk next dc, dc in next dc, [ch 5, sl st in next ch-5 sp] 4 times, ch 5**, dc in next dc, rep from * around, ending last rep at **, join. *(8 groups of 14 dc)*

Rnd 19: Ch 3, *sk next dc, dc in each of next 4 dc, sk next 2 dc, dc in each of next 4 dc, sk next dc, dc in next dc, [ch 5, sl st in next ch-5 sp] 5 times, ch 5**, dc in next dc, rep from * around, ending last rep at **, join. *(8 groups of 10 dc)*

Rnd 20: Ch 3, *sk next dc, dc in each of next 2 dc, sk next 2 dc, dc in each of next 2 dc, sk next dc, dc in next dc, [ch 5, sl st in next ch-5 sp] 6 times, ch 5**, dc in next dc, rep from * around, ending last rep at **, join. *(8 groups of 6 dc; 56 ch-5 sps)*

Rnd 21: Ch 3, sk next dc, dc in each of next 2 dc, sk next dc, dc in next dc, [ch 5, sl st in next ch-5 sp] 7 times, ch 5**, dc in next dc, rep from * around, ending last rep at **, join. *(8 groups of 4 dc; 64 ch-5 sps)*

Rnd 22: Ch 3, *sk next 2 dc, dc in next dc, [ch 5, sl st in next ch-5 sp] 8 times, ch 5**, dc in next dc, rep from * around, ending last rep at **, join. *(8 groups of 2 dc; 72 ch-5 sps)*

Rnd 23: Sl st to third ch of ch-5 sp, 11 dc in next ch-5 sp, *sl st in third ch of next ch-5 sp, ch 7**, sl st in third ch of next ch-5 sp, 11 dc in next ch-5 sp, rep from * around, ending last rep at **, join with sl st in first dc. *(24 groups of 11 dc)*

Rnd 24: Ch 4 *(counts as first tr)*, tr in each of next 4 dc, *(tr, ch 3, tr) in next dc, tr in each of next 5 dc, sl st in next ch-7 sp**, tr in each of next 5 dc, rep from * around, ending last rep at **, join with sl st in fourth ch of beg ch-4.

Rnd 25: Sl st to fourth tr, *ch 5, ({**pc**–see Special Stitches, ch 5} twice, pc) in next ch-3 sp, ch 5, sk next 2 tr, sl st in next tr, ch-5, sl st in next sl st, ch 5**, sk next 3 tr, sl st in next tr, rep from * around, ending last rep at **, join with sl st in base of beg ch-5. Fasten off.❏❏

Ruffled Lace Tissue Box Cover

Design by Jo Ann Maxwell

SKILL LEVEL
■■■□ INTERMEDIATE

FINISHED SIZE
Fits boutique-style tissue box

MATERIALS
- J. & P. Coats South Maid crochet cotton size 10 (350 yds per ball):
    1 ball #42 cream
- Size 5/1.90mm steel crochet hook or size needed to obtain gauge
- 4 pink 1¼-inch-wide ribbon roses with leaves
- White pearls:
    ⅛-inch-diameter: 4
    ¼-inch-diameter: 8
- 3¾ yds ¼-inch-wide green satin ribbon
- Glue gun
- Plastic wrap
- Spray starch

GAUGE
First 3 rnds = 3¼ inches in diameter

SPECIAL STITCHES
Beginning shell (beg shell): (Ch 3—*counts as first dc,* dc, ch 2, 2 dc) in indicated ch sp.
Shell: (2 dc, ch 2, 2 dc) in indicated ch sp.
Beginning double shell (beg dbl shell): (Beg shell, ch 2, 2 dc) in indicated ch sp.
Double shell (dbl shell): (Shell, ch 2, 2 dc) in indicated sp.

INSTRUCTIONS
COVER
Rnd 1: Beg at bottom, ch 4, sl st in first ch to form ring, ch 3 *(counts as first dc throughout),* 23 dc in ring, join with sl st in third ch of beg ch-3. *(24 dc)*
Rnd 2: Ch 7 *(counts as first dtr and ch-2),* (dtr, ch 2) in each dc around, join with sl st in fifth ch of beg ch-7. *(24 ch-2 sps)*
Rnd 3: Ch 3, [dc in each of next 2 chs, dc in next dtr] around, ending with dc in each of last 2 chs, join with sl st in third ch of beg ch-3. *(72 dc)*
Rnd 4: Ch 1, sc in first st, ch 4, [sk next dc, sc in next dc, ch 4] around, join with sl st in beg sc. *(36 ch-4 sps)*
Rnds 5–8: Sl st in each of next 2 chs, ch 1, sc in same ch sp, ch 4, [sc in next ch-4 sp, ch 4] around, join.
Rnd 9: Sl st in next ch-4 sp, **beg dbl shell** *(see Special Stitches)* in same ch sp, *ch 3, sc in next ch-4 sp, [ch 4, sc in next ch-4 sp] 7 times, ch 3**, **dbl shell** *(see Special Stitches)* in next ch-4 sp, rep from * around, ending last rep at **, join.
Rnd 10: Sl st in next dc and in ch-2 sp, **beg shell** *(see Special Stitches)* in same ch sp, ch 3, **shell** *(see Special Stitches)* in next ch-2 sp, *ch 3, sk next ch-3 sp, sc in

16 A Passion For Pineapples • Annie's Attic, Berne, IN 46711 • AnniesAttic.com

next ch-4 sp, [ch 4, sc in next ch-4 sp] 6 times**, [ch 3, shell in next ch-2 sp] twice, rep from * around, ending last rep at **, ch 3, join.

Rnd 11: Sl st in next dc and in ch-2 sp, beg shell in same ch sp, *ch 3, 7 dc in next ch-3 sp, ch 3, shell in next shell, ch 3, sk next ch-3 sp, sc in next ch-4 sp, [ch 4, sc in next ch-4 sp] 5 times, ch 3**, shell in next shell, rep from * around, ending last rep at **, join.

Rnd 12: Sl st in next dc and in ch-2 sp, beg shell in same ch sp, *ch 3, sc in next ch-3 sp, dc in next dc, [ch 1, dc in next dc] 6 times, sc in next ch-3 sp, ch 3, shell in next shell, ch 3, sk next ch-3 sp, sc in next ch-4 sp, [ch 4, sc in next ch-4 sp] 4 times, ch 3**, shell in next shell, rep from * around, ending last rep at **, join.

Rnd 13: Sl st in next dc and in ch-2 sp, beg shell in same ch sp, *ch 3, sk next ch-3 sp, [sc in next dc, ch 3] 7 times, shell in next shell, ch 3, sk next ch-3 sp, sc in next ch-4 sp, [ch 4, sc in next ch-4 sp] 3 times, ch 3**, shell in next shell, rep from * around, ending last rep at **, join.

Rnd 14: Sl st in next dc and in ch-2 sp, beg shell in same ch sp, *ch 3, sk next ch-3 sp, [sc in next ch-3 sp, ch 3] 6 times, shell in next shell, ch 3, sk next ch-3 sp, sc in next ch-4 sp, [ch 4, sc in next ch-4 sp] twice, ch 3**, shell in next shell, rep from * around, ending last rep at **, join.

Rnd 15: Sl st in next dc and in ch-2 sp, beg shell in same ch sp, *ch 3, sk next ch-3 sp, [sc in next ch-3 sp, ch 3] 5 times, shell in next shell, ch 4, sc in next ch-3 sp, [ch 4, sc in next ch-4 sp] twice, ch 4, sc in next ch-3 sp, ch 4**, shell in next shell, rep from * around, ending last rep at **, join.

Rnd 16: Sl st in next dc and in ch-2 sp, beg shell in same ch sp, *ch 3, sk next ch-3 sp, [sc in next ch-3 sp, ch 3] 4 times, shell in next shell, ch 4, [sc in next ch-4 sp, ch 4] 5 times**, shell in next shell, rep from * around, ending last rep at **, join.

Rnd 17: Sl st in next dc and in ch-2 sp, beg shell in same ch sp, *ch 3, sk next ch-3 sp, [sc in next ch-3 sp, ch 3] 3 times, shell in next shell, ch 4, [sc in next ch-4 sp, ch 4] 6 times**, shell in next shell, rep from * around, ending last rep at **, join.

Rnd 18: Sl st in next dc and in ch-2 sp, beg shell in same ch sp, *ch 3, sk next ch-3 sp, [sc in next ch-3 sp, ch 3] twice, shell in next shell, ch 4, [sc in next ch-4 sp, ch 4] 7 times**, shell in next shell, rep from * around, ending last rep at **, join.

Rnd 19: Sl st in next dc and in ch-2 sp, beg shell in same ch sp, *ch 3, sk next ch-3 sp, sc in next ch-3 sp, ch 3, shell in next shell, ch 4, [sc in next ch-4 sp, ch 4] 8 times**, shell in next shell sp, rep from * around, ending last rep at **, join.

Rnd 20: Sl st in next dc and in ch-2 sp, beg shell in same ch sp, shell in next shell, *ch 4, [sc in next ch-4 sp, ch 4] 9 times**, shell in each of next 2 shells, rep from * around, ending last rep at **, join.

Rnd 21: Sl st in next dc and in ch-2 sp, ch 1, sc in same ch sp, sc in ch sp of next shell, *ch 4, [sc in next ch-4 sp, ch 4] 10 times**, [sc in ch sp of next shell] twice, rep from * around, ending last rep at **, join with sl st in beg sc.

Rnd 22: Sl st in next sc and in each of next 2 chs, ch 1, sc in same ch sp, ch 4, [sc in next ch-4 sp, ch 4] around, join. *(44 ch-4 sps)*

Rnds 23–27: Sl st in each of next 2 chs, ch 1, sc in same ch sp, ch 4, [sc in next ch-4 sp, ch 4] around, join.

Rnd 28: Sl st in each of next 2 chs, ch 6 *(counts as first dc, ch-3)*, [dc in next ch-4 sp, ch 3] around, join with sl st in third ch of beg ch-6.

Rnd 29: Ch 1, sc in first st, ch 4, [sc in next ch-3 sp, ch 4, sc in next dc, ch 4] around, ending with sc in last ch-3 sp, ch 4, join. *(88 ch-4 sps)*

Rnds 30–35: Sl st in each of next 2 chs, ch 1, sc in same ch sp, ch 4, [sc in next ch-4 sp, ch 4] around, join.

Rnd 36: Sl st in next ch, ch 5 *(counts as first dc and ch-2)*, *[dc in next ch, ch 2] 3 times, sc in next ch-4 sp, ch 2**, dc in first ch of next ch-4, ch 2, rep from * around, ending last rep at **, join with sl st in third ch of beg ch-5. Fasten off.

FINISHING

1. Cover tissue box with plastic wrap; place crocheted cover over box, centering pineapples over 4 sides. Gather top with string woven through ch sps of rnd 28. Pull string snugly, leaving sp for tissue to come out. Shape ruffle; spray with starch. Let dry.
2. Remove crocheted cover. Cut four 24-inch lengths of ribbon. Beg at top of each pineapple, weave ribbon through sps at outer edge of shells around each of four pineapples; tie in bow at top and trim ends.
3. Glue satin rose to center of each bow. Glue two small pearls and one large pearl at base of each pineapple over dbl shell.
4. Place cover on box, centering pineapples over four sides. Weave rem piece of ribbon through ch sps of rnd 28; gather and tie in bow. Trim ends to desired length.

Peppermint Poinsettia

Design by Agnes Russell

SKILL LEVEL
■■☐☐ EASY

FINISHED SIZE
21 inches in diameter

MATERIALS
- ❏ J. & P. Coats Knit-Cro-Sheen crochet cotton size 10:
    100 yds #453 shaded Christmas
    300 yds #126 Spanish red
- ❏ Size 8/1.50mm steel crochet hook or size needed to obtain gauge
- ❏ Tapestry needle
- ❏ Spray starch

GAUGE
3 shell rnds = 1 inch

SPECIAL STITCHES
Beginning shell (beg shell): Sl st across to indicated ch sp, ch 3 *(counts as first dc)*, (dc, ch 3, 2 dc) in same ch sp.
Shell: (2 dc, ch 3, 2 dc) in indicated ch sp.
Beginning Double shell (beg dbl shell): (Ch 3, dc, ch 3, 2 dc, ch 3, 2 dc) in indicated ch sp.
Double shell (dbl shell): (2 dc, ch 3, 2 dc, ch 3, 2 dc) in indicated ch sp.

INSTRUCTIONS
INNER PINEAPPLE RING
Rnd 1: With shaded Christmas, ch 8, sl st in first ch to form ring, ch 1, 20 sc in ring, join with sl st in beg sc. *(20 sc)*
Rnd 2: Ch 1, sc in first sc, ch 2, [sc in next sc, ch 2] around, join. *(20 ch-2 sps)*
Rnd 3: Sl st into ch-2 sp, ch 1, sc in same ch-2 sp, ch 2, [sc in next ch-2 sp, ch 2] around, join.
Rnd 4: Sl st into ch-2 sp, ch 1, sc in same ch-2 sp, ch 3, [sc in next ch-2 sp, ch 3] around, join.
Rnd 5: Sl st into ch-3 sp, ch 1, sc in same ch-3 sp, ch 3, [sc in next ch-3 sp, ch 3] around, join.
Rnd 6: Sl st into ch-3 sp, ch 1, sc in same ch-3 sp, ch 4, [sc in next ch-3 sp, ch 4] around, join.
Rnd 7: Beg shell *(see Special Stitches)* in first ch-4 sp, **shell** *(see Special Stitches)* in each ch-4 sp around, join with sl st in top of beg ch-3. *(20 shells)*
Rnd 8: Beg shell in shell, ch 1, [shell in shell, ch 1] around, join.
Rnd 9: Beg shell in shell, ch 2, [shell in shell, ch 2] around, join. Fasten off.
Rnd 10: Join Spanish red with sl st in any ch-3 sp of shell, beg shell in same ch sp, ch 2, 10 dc in next ch-3 sp of shell, ch 2, [shell in shell, ch 2, 10 dc in next ch-3 sp of shell, ch 2] around, join with sl st in top of beg ch-3. *(10 pineapples started)*
Rnd 11: Beg shell, ch 2, dc in first dc of 10-dc group, [ch 1, dc in next dc] 9 times, ch 2, *shell in shell, ch 2, dc in first dc of 10-dc group, [ch 1, dc in next dc] 9 times, ch 2, rep from * around, join.
Rnd 12: Beg shell in shell, *ch 2, sc in next ch-1 sp, [ch 3, sc in next ch-1 sp] 8 times, ch 2**, shell in shell, rep from * around, ending last rep at **, join.
Rnd 13: Beg shell in shell, *ch 2, sc in next ch-3 sp, [ch 3, sc in next ch-3 sp] 7 times, ch 2**, shell in shell, rep from * around, ending last rep at **, join.
Rnd 14: Beg dbl shell *(see*

Special Stitches) in shell, *ch 2, sc in next ch-3 sp, [ch 3, sc in next ch-3 sp] 6 times, ch 2, **dbl shell** (*see Special Stitches*), rep from * around, ending last rep at **, join, sl st across shell and into second ch-3 sp of dbl shell.

INNER PINEAPPLE FINISHING
Row 15: Beg shell in shell, ch 2, sc in next ch-3 sp, [ch 3, sc in next ch-3 sp] 5 times, ch 2, shell in shell, turn.
Row 16: Beg shell in shell, ch 2, sc in next ch-3 sp, [ch 3, sc in next ch-3 sp] 4 times, ch 2, shell in shell, turn.
Row 17: Beg shell in shell, ch 2, sc in next ch-3 sp, [ch 3, sc in next ch-3 sp] 3 times, ch 2, shell in shell, turn.
Row 18: Beg shell in shell, ch 2, sc in next ch-3 sp, [ch 3, sc in next ch-3 sp] twice, ch 2, shell in shell, turn.
Row 19: Beg shell in shell, ch 2, sc in next ch-3 sp, ch 3, sc in next ch-3 sp, ch 2, shell in shell, turn.
Row 20: Beg shell in shell, ch 2, sc in rem ch-3 sp, ch 2, shell in shell. Fasten off.
Next rows: *With finished pineapple to the right, join Spanish red in next unworked ch-3 sp of shell of rnd 28, rep rows 15–20.
Rep from * around until all 10 pineapples are completed.
At the end of 10th pineapple turn, **do not fasten off.**

PINEAPPLE JOINING
Note: Rnd 21 is crocheted in rem 2 shells of each pineapple around row 20.

Rnd 21: Sl st into ch-3 sp of shell, beg shell in shell, *ch 2, shell in shell, ch 23** shell in shell rep from * around, ending last rep at **, join. Fasten off.

OUTER PINEAPPLE RING
Rnd 22: Join shaded Christmas with sl st in first shell of previous rnd, beg shell in shell, *ch 2, shell in shell, [ch 2, sk next 5 chs, shell in next ch] 3 times, ch 2, sk next 5 chs**, shell in shell, rep from * around, ending last rep at **, join. (50 shells)
Rnd 23: Beg shell in shell, *ch 2, sc in ch-2 sp, ch 2**, shell in shell, rep from * around, ending last rep at **, join.
Rnd 24: Beg shell in shell, [ch 3, shell in shell] around, ch 3, join.
Rnd 25: Beg shell in shell, *ch 3, sc in ch-3 sp, ch 3**, shell in shell, rep from * around, ending last rep at **, join. Fasten off.
Rnd 26: Join Spanish red with sl st in ch-3 sp of first shell, beg shell in shell, *ch 2, 7 dc in next ch-3 sp of shell, ch 2**, shell in shell, rep from * around, ending last rep at **, join.
Rnd 27: Beg shell in shell, *ch 2, dc in first dc of 7-dc group, [ch 1, dc in next dc] 6 times, ch 2**, shell in shell, rep from * around, ending last rep at **, join.
Rnd 28: Beg dbl shell in shell, *ch 2, sc in next ch-1 sp, [ch 3, sc in next ch-1 sp] 5 times, ch 2** dbl shell in shell, rep from * around, ending last rep at **, join, sl st across shell and into second ch-3 sp of beg dbl shell.

OUTER PINEAPPLE FINISHING
Row 29: Beg shell in shell, ch 2, sc in next ch-3 sp, [ch 3, sc in next ch-3 sp] 4 times, ch 2, shell in shell, turn.
Row 30: Beg shell in shell, ch 2, sc in next ch-3 sp, [ch 3, sc in next ch-3 sp] 3 times, ch 2, shell in shell, turn.
Row 31: Beg shell in shell, ch 2, sc in next ch-3 sp, [ch 3, sc in next ch-3 sp] twice, ch 2, shell in shell, turn.
Row 32: Beg shell in shell, ch 2, sc in next ch-3 sp, ch 3, sc in next ch-3 sp, shell in shell, turn.
Row 33: Beg shell in shell, ch 2, sc in ch-3 sp, ch 2, shell in shell. Fasten off.
Next rows: *With finished pineapple to the right, join Spanish red with sl st in next unworked ch-3 sp of shell on rnd 28, rep rows 29–33. Rep from * until a total of 25 pineapples are completed.
At the end of the last pineapple, **do not fasten off,** turn, sl st back into ch-3 sp of last shell, turn.

TRIM
Rnd 34: Ch 1,*sc in ch-3 sp of shell, [ch 4, sc in side of dc] 5 times, ch 4, sc in sp between dc sts of rnd 28 *(center of dc sts of dbl shell),* [ch 4, sc in side of dc] 5 times, ch 4, sc in ch-3 sp of shell, ch 4, rep from * around, join. Fasten off.

FINISHING
Place doily on padded flat surface, spray with starch, press with steam iron. Allow to dry completely.❑❑

Pineapple Vest

Design by Nazanin Fard

SKILL LEVEL
INTERMEDIATE

FINISHED SIZE
Lady's 32–34-inch bust

FINISHED GARMENT MEASUREMENT
36 inches

MATERIALS
- Crochet cotton size 10: 1,105 yds ecru
- Size 5/1.90mm steel crochet hook or size needed to obtain gauge
- Tapestry needle
- Sewing needle
- ¾-inch ecru shank button
- Ecru sewing thread

GAUGE
7 dc = 1 inch
Check gauge to save time.

SPECIAL STITCH
Shell: (2 dc, ch 3, 2 dc) in next st or ch sp.

INSTRUCTIONS
UPPER BODY
Row 1: Beg **at neck,** ch 188, 4 dc in fourth ch from hook *(first 3 chs count as first dc)*, *ch 1, sk next 4 chs, sc in next ch, ch 3, sk next 3 chs, sc in next ch, ch 4, sk next 4 chs, sc in next ch, ch 3, sk next 3 chs, sc in next ch, ch 1, sk next 4 chs**, 9 dc in next ch, rep from * across, ending last rep at **, 5 dc in last ch, turn.

Row 2: Ch 4 *(counts as first dc and ch-1 sp)*, [dc in next dc, ch 1] 4 times, *sk next sc, **shell** (see Special Stitch) in each of next 2 sc, ch 1**, [dc in next dc, ch 1] 9 times, rep from * across, ending last rep at **, [dc in next dc, ch 1] 4 times, dc in last st, turn.

Row 3: Ch 4, [sc in next ch-1 sp, ch 3] 4 times, *2 dc in ch sp of next shell, ch 1, 2 dc in ch sp of next shell, ch 3, sk next ch-1 sp**, [sc in next ch-1 sp, ch 3] 8 times, rep from * across, ending last rep at **, [sc in next ch-1 sp, ch 3] 3 times, sc in last ch sp, turn.

Row 4: Ch 4, [sc in next ch-3 sp, ch 3] 3 times, *shell in next ch-1 sp, ch 3, sk next ch-3 sp**, [sc in next ch-3 sp, ch 3] 7 times, rep from * across, ending last rep at **, [sc in next ch-3 sp, ch 3] 3 times, sc in last ch sp, turn.

Row 5: Ch 4, [sc in next ch-3 sp, ch 3] 3 times, *shell in next shell, ch 3, sk next ch-3 sp**, [sc in next ch-3 sp, ch 3] 6 times, rep from * across, ending last rep at **, [sc in next ch-3 sp, ch 3] twice, sc in last ch sp, turn.

Row 6: Ch 4, [sc in next ch-3 sp, ch 3] twice, *sk next ch-3 sp, ({2 dc, ch 1} twice, 2 dc) in next shell, ch 3, sk next ch-3 sp**, [sc in next ch-3 sp, ch 3] 5 times, rep from * across, ending last rep at **, [sc in next ch-3 sp, ch 3] twice, sc in last ch sp, turn.

Row 7: Ch 4, [sc in next ch-3 sp, ch 3] twice, *sk next ch-3 sp, shell in next ch-1 sp, ch 1, shell in next ch-1 sp, ch 3, sk next ch-3 sp**, [sc in next ch-3 sp, ch 3] 4 times, rep from * across, ending last rep at **, sc in next ch-3 sp, ch 3, sc in last ch sp, turn.

Row 8: Ch 4, sc in next ch-3 sp, ch 3, *sk next ch-3 sp, shell in next shell, ch 1, shell in next ch-1 sp, ch 1, shell in next shell, ch 3, sk next ch-3 sp**, [sc in next ch-3 sp, ch 3] 3 times, rep from * across, ending last rep at **, sc in next ch-3 sp, ch 3, sc in last ch sp, turn.

Row 9: Ch 4, sc in next ch-3 sp, ch 3*, sk next ch-3 sp, [shell in next shell, ch 2] twice, shell in next shell, ch 3, sk next ch-3 sp**, [sc in next ch-3 sp, ch 3] twice, rep from * across, ending last rep at **, sc in last ch sp, turn.

Row 10: Ch 5 *(counts as first dc and ch-2 sp)*, *sk next ch-3 sp, shell in next shell, ch 2, 9 dc in next shell, ch 2, shell in next shell**, ch 3, sk next ch-3 sp, sc in next ch-3 sp, ch 3, rep from * across, ending last rep at **, ch 2, dc in last ch sp, turn.

Row 11: Ch 3, *shell in next shell, ch 1, sk next ch-2 sp, [dc in next dc, ch 1] 9 times, shell in next shell, rep from * across, ending with dc in third ch of ch-5, turn.

Row 12: Ch 3, *2 dc in next shell, ch 3, sk next ch-1 sp, [sc in next ch-1 sp, ch 3] 8 times, 2 dc in next shell**, ch 1, rep from * across, ending last rep at **, dc in last st, turn.

Row 13: Ch 3, 2 dc in next dc, *ch 3, sk next ch-3 sp, [sc in next ch-3 sp, ch 3] 7 times**, shell in next ch-1 sp, rep from * across, ending last rep at **, sk next ch-3 sp and next dc, 2 dc next dc, dc in last st, turn.

Row 14: Ch 3, 2 dc in sp between next 2 dc, *ch 3, sk next ch-3 sp, [sc in next ch-3 sp, ch 3] 6 times, sk next ch-3 sp**, shell in next shell, rep from * across, ending last rep at **, 2 dc in sp between next 2 dc, dc in last st, turn.

Rnd 15: Ch 3, 2 sc in sp between next 2 dc, *ch 3, sk next ch-3 sp, [sc in next ch-3 sp, ch 3] 5 times, sk next ch-3 sp**, ({2 dc, 1} twice, 2 dc) in next shell, rep from * across, ending last rep at **, 2 dc between next 2 dc, dc in last st, turn.

Row 16: Ch 3, shell in sp between next 2 dc, *ch 3, sk next ch-3 sp, [sc in next ch-3 sp, ch 3] 4 times**, shell in next ch-1 sp, ch 1, shell in next ch-1 sp, rep from * across, ending last rep at **, sk next ch-3 sp, shell in sp between next 2 dc, dc in last st, turn.

Rnd 17: Ch 3, shell in next shell, *ch 3, sk next ch-3 sp, [sc in next ch-3 sp, ch 3] 3 times, sk next ch-3 sp, shell in next shell**, ch 1, shell in next ch-1 sp, ch 1, shell in next shell, rep from * across, ending last rep at **, dc in last st, turn.

Rnd 18: Ch 5, shell in next shell, *ch 3, sk next ch-3 sp, [sc in next ch-3 sp, ch 3] twice, sk next ch-3 sp**, [shell in next shell, ch 2] twice, shell in next shell, rep from * across, ending last rep **, shell in next shell, ch 2, dc in last st, turn.

Row 19: Ch 3, 4 dc in first dc, ch 2, *shell in next shell, ch 3, sk next ch-3 sp, sc in next ch-3 sp, ch 3, sk next ch-3 sp, shell in next shell, ch 2**, 9 dc in next shell, ch 2, rep from * across, ending last rep at **, 5 dc in last st, turn.

Row 20: Ch 4, [dc in next dc, ch 1] 4 times, *shell in each of next 2 shells, ch 1, sk next ch-2 sp**, [dc in next dc, ch 1] 9 times, rep from * across, ending last rep at **, [dc in next dc, ch 1] 4 times, dc in last st, turn.

Rows 21–36: Rep rows 3–18. Fasten off at end of last row.

UPPER RIGHT FRONT

Row 1: Beg at shoulder edge and working toward neck, working in starting ch on opposite side of row 1 on Upper Back, join with sl st in first ch, (ch 3, 4 dc) in same ch, *ch 1, sk next 4 chs, sc in next ch, ch 3, sk next 3 chs, sc in next ch, ch 4, sk next 4 chs, sc in next ch, ch 3, sk next 3 chs, sc in next ch, ch 1, sk next 4 chs*, 9 dc in next ch, rep between * once, 5 dc in last ch, turn.

Rows 2–27: Rep rows 2–27 of Upper Back.

Row 28: Ch 43, sc in seventh ch from hook, ch 1, sk next 4 chs, 9 dc in next ch, ch 1, sk next 4 chs, sc in next ch, [ch 3, sk next 3 chs, sc in next ch] 3 times, ch 1, sk next 4 chs, dc in next ch, ch 1, sk next 4 chs, sc in next ch, ch 3, sk next 3 chs, sc in next ch, ch 2, *shell in next shell, ch 2, 9 dc in next shell, ch 2, shell in next shell*, ch 3, sk next ch-3 sp, sc in next ch-3 sp, ch 3, rep between * once, ch 2, sk next ch-3 sp, sc in last ch sp, turn.

Row 29: Ch 3, [shell in next shell, ch 1, sk next ch-2 sp, (dc, ch 1) in each of next 9 dc, shell in next shell] twice, shell in next sc, *ch 1, sk next ch-3 sp, (dc, ch 1) in each of next 9 dc*, sk next sc, shell in each of next 2 sc, rep between * once, shell in next sc, sk next 3 chs, dc in next ch, turn.

Rows 30–35: Rep rows 12–17 of Upper Back.

Row 36: Rep row 18 of Upper Back, join with sl st in top of first st of last row on Upper Back. Fasten off.

UPPER LEFT FRONT

Rows 1–36: Rep rows 1–36 of Upper Right Front.

JOINING FRONTS & BACK

Row 37: With WS facing, join with sl st in top of first st at front opening on last row of Upper Right Front, rep row 19 of Upper Back across, working 9 dc in each joining st between Upper Right Front and Back and Upper Left Front and Back at underarms.

Row 38: Rep row 20 of Upper Back.

Rows 39–83: Rep rows 3–20 of Upper Back consecutively, ending with row 11. Fasten off at end of last row.

FRONT EDGING

Row 1: With WS facing, join with sc end of row at bottom of left front opening, 2 sc in same row, 3 sc in end of each row up to last row before neck shaping, 4 sc in next row, sc evenly sp across neck opening to first row of neck shaping at top of right front opening, 4 sc in end of next row, 3 sc in end of each row down to bottom corner of right front opening, turn.

Row 2: Ch 1, sc in each st across. Fasten off.

ARMHOLE EDGING

Rnd 1: With RS facing, join with sc in st at underarm, sc evenly sp around armhole, join with sl st in beg sc.

Rnd 2: Ch 1, sc in each st around, join in beg sc. Fasten off.

Sew button to edging on upper left front *(see photo)*.❏❏

Pineapple Ornament

Design by Jo Ann Maxwell

SKILL LEVEL
■■■□ INTERMEDIATE

FINISHED SIZE
5½ inches tall x 4 inches wide

MATERIALS
- Crochet cotton size 10:
    50 yds cream
- Size 5/1.90mm crochet hook
- Nylon thread
- Beads:
    3mm pearl: 5
    9 x 20mm pearl drop: 1
- Ribbon:
    1 yd ⅜-inch blue double-faced feather-edge
    12 inches ⅛-inch teal satin ribbon
- 3 antique rose ⅝-inch ribbon roses
- 6 sprigs dried statice
- Glue gun
- Fabric stiffener

SPECIAL STITCH
Shell: (2 dc, ch 2, 2 dc) in indicated sp.

INSTRUCTIONS
PINEAPPLE
Row 1: Ch 5, sl st in first ch to form ring, ch 3 *(counts as first dc)*, dc in ring, [ch 2, 2 dc in ring] 3 times, turn. *(8 dc, 4 ch-2 sps)*

Row 2: Ch 3, **shell** *(see Special Stitch)* in first ch-2 sp, 10 dc in next ch-2 sp, shell in last ch-2 sp, turn.
Row 3: Ch 3, shell in shell, [dc in next dc, ch 2] 9 times, dc in next dc, shell in next shell, turn.
Row 4: Ch 3, shell in shell, ch 2, sc in next dc, [ch 3, sc in next dc] 9 times, ch 2, shell in next shell, turn.
Rows 5–12: Ch 3, shell in shell, ch 2, (sc, ch 3) in each ch-3 sp across to last ch-3 sp, sc in last sp, ch 2, shell in last shell, turn.
Row 13: Ch 3, shell in shell, ch 2, sc in ch-3 sp, ch 2, shell in last shell, turn.
Row 14: Ch 3, shell in each of next 2 shells. Fasten off.

FINISHING
1. Stiffen Pineapple, shape and let dry.
2. Tie pearl drop at bottom of Pineapple with nylon thread as shown in photo.
3. Begin at top, weave ⅜-inch-wide blue ribbon from back of Pineapple through beading (ch-2 sps); secure one end with glue. Leave 4-inch length of ribbon at back; glue end over ribbon end at beg to form loop for hanging.
4. Make bow from 6-inch length of ⅜-inch-wide blue ribbon; glue over bottom two shells. Make another bow from 9-inch length of blue ribbon; glue at top of pineapple.
5. Glue three or four sprigs of statice below bow at top. Glue two ribbon roses over statice.
6. Glue two or three sprigs of statice at bottom point of woven ribbon. Glue one ribbon rose over statice.
7. Cut ⅛-inch-wide teal ribbon into eight pieces ranging in length from 1 to 1½ inches. Form into individual lps and glue five lps around top roses and three lps around bottom rose.
8. Glue three pearls around roses at top; glue two pearls around rose at bottom. ❏❏

Pineapple Waves Edging

SKILL LEVEL
■■■□ INTERMEDIATE

FINISHED SIZE
Fits standard-size pillowcase

MATERIALS
- Crochet cotton size 10:
    438 yds white
- Size 10/1.15mm steel crochet hook or size needed to obtain gauge
- Tapestry needle
- Sewing needle
- Ribbon:
    ⅔ yd ⅝-wide
- Sewing thread to match ribbon

GAUGE
11 sts = 1 inch, dc = ¼ inch

SPECIAL STITCH
Shell: (2 dc, ch 2, 2 dc) next ch or ch sp.

INSTRUCTIONS
EDGING
Row 1: Ch 55, sc in eighth ch from hook, [ch 5, sk next 3 chs, dc in next ch] twice, ch 7, sk next 4 chs, dc in next ch, [ch 5, sk next

3 chs, sc in next ch] 5 times, [ch 5, sk next 4 chs, sc in next ch] twice, ch 5, sk next 3 chs, **shell** *(see Special Stitch)* in last ch, turn. *(12 ch sps, 1 shell)*

Row 2 (RS): Ch 7, shell in ch sp of shell, ch 5, sk next ch sp, dc in next ch sp, ch 7, dc in next ch sp, ch 5, sk next ch sp, shell in next ch sp, ch 5, [sc in next ch sp, ch 5] 3 times, 10 sc in next ch sp, [ch 5, sc in next ch sp] 3 times, turn. *(10 sc, 10 ch sps, 2 shells)*

Row 3: Ch 7, sc in first ch sp, ch 5, sc in next ch sp, ch 5, dc in next ch sp, ch 7, dc next ch sp, ch 5, [sc in next ch sp, ch 5] 3 times, shell in next shell, ch 5, sk next ch sp, 17 dc in next ch sp, ch 5, shell in last shell, turn. *(17 dc, 10 ch sps, 2 shells)*

Row 4: Ch 7, shell in first shell, ch 5, sk next ch sp and next dc, sc in **back lps** *(see Stitch Guide)* of each of next 15 sts, ch 5, sk next dc and ch sp, shell in next shell, ch 5, [sc in next ch sp, ch 5] 4 times, 10 sc in next ch sp, [ch 5, sc in next ch sp] 3 times, turn.

Row 5: Ch 7, sc in first ch sp, ch 5, sc in next ch sp, ch 5, dc in next ch sp, ch 7, dc in next ch sp, ch 5, [sc in next ch sp, ch 5] 4 times, shell in next shell, ch 5, sk next ch sp and next sc, sc in next sc, [ch 2, sc in next sc] 13 times, ch 5, shell in last shell, turn.

Row 6: Ch 7, shell in first shell, ch 5, sk next 2 ch sps, sc in next ch sp, [ch 2, sc in next ch sp] 11 times, ch 5, shell in next shell, ch 5, [sc in next ch sp, ch 5] 5 times, 10 sc in next ch sp, [ch 5, sc in next ch sp] 3 times, turn

Row 7: Ch 7, sc in first ch sp, ch 5, sc in next ch sp, ch 5, dc in next ch sp, ch 7, dc in next ch sp, ch 5, [sc in next ch sp, ch 5] 5 times, shell in next shell, ch 5, sk next 2 ch sps, sc in next ch sp, [ch 2, sc in next ch sp] 9 times, ch 5, shell in last shell, turn.

Row 8: Ch 7, shell in first shell, ch 5, sk next 2 ch sps, sc in next ch sp, [ch 2, sc in next ch sp] 7 times, ch 5, shell in next shell, ch 5, [sc in next ch sp, ch 5] 6 times, 10 sc in next ch sp, [ch 5, sc in next ch sp] 3 times, turn.

Row 9: Ch 7, sc in first ch sp, ch 5, sc in next ch sp, ch 5, dc in next ch sp, ch 7, dc in next ch sp, ch 5, [sc in next ch sp, ch 5] 6 times, shell in next shell, ch 5, sk next 2 ch sps, sc in next ch sp, [ch 2, sc in next ch sp] 5 times, ch 5, shell in last shell, turn.

Row 10: Ch 7, shell in first shell, ch 5, sk next 2 ch sps, sc in next ch sp, [ch 2, sc in next ch sp] 3 times, ch 5, shell in next shell, ch 5, [sc in next ch sp, ch 5] 7 times, 10 sc in next ch sp, [ch 5, sc in next ch sp] 3 times, turn.

Row 11: Ch 7, sc in first ch sp, ch 5, sc in next ch sp, ch 5, dc in next ch sp, ch 7, dc in next ch sp, ch 5, [sc in next ch sp, ch 5] 7 times, shell in next shell, ch 5, sk next 2 ch sps, sc in next ch sp, ch 5, shell in last shell, turn.

Row 12: Ch 7, shell in first shell, shell in next shell, ch 5, [sc in next ch sp, ch 5] 8 times, 10 sc in next ch sp, [ch 5, sc in next ch sp] 3 times, turn

Row 13: Ch 7, sc in first ch sp, ch 5, sc in next ch sp, ch 5, dc in next ch sp, ch 7, dc in next ch sp, ch 5, [sc in next ch sp, ch 5] 7 times, shell in next shell, sc in next ch sp, turn.

Next rows: Rep rows 2–13, 13 more times, or until piece measures 44 inches. Fasten off at end of last row.

Sew first and last rows tog. With RS facing you, work 10 sc over seam in same manner as other rows. Fasten off.

Starting at seam, join with sc in end of last row, sc in same row, 11 sc in next ch-7 sp, [2 sc in end of next row, 11 sc in next ch-7 sp] around, join with sl st in beg sc. Fasten off.

Weave ribbon through 10-sc sps. Sew ends tog.

Sew over hem of pillowcase as desired.

Grandma's Delight

SKILL LEVEL
INTERMEDIATE

FINISHED SIZES
Doily: 20 inches in diameter
Napkin: 13 inches square

MATERIALS
- Crochet cotton size 40 (400 yds per ball):
  3 balls white
- 12/1.00mm steel crochet hook or size needed to obtain gauge
- 12-inch square piece of linen

SPECIAL STITCHES
Beginning popcorn (beg pc): Ch 3, 4 dc in same ch sp, drop lp from hook, insert hook in top of ch-3, pull dropped lp through.
Popcorn (pc): 5 dc in next st or ch sp, drop lp from hook, insert hook in first st of 5-dc group, pull dropped lp through.
Beginning shell (beg shell): (Sl st, beg pc, ch 5, pc) in first ch-sp.
Shell: (Pc, ch 5, pc) in next ch sp.
Treble decrease (tr dec): (Yo twice, insert hook, yo, pull lp through, [yo, pull through 2 lps on hook] twice) in each of the sts or ch sps indicated yo, pull through all lps on hook.

INSTRUCTIONS
DOILY

Rnd 1 (RS): Ch 10, sl st in first ch to form ring, ch 1, 20 sc in ring, join with sl st in beg sc. *(20 sc)*

Rnd 2: Ch 1, sc in first st, ch 3, sk next st, [sc in next st, ch 3, sk next st] around, join. *(10 sc, 10 ch sps)*

Rnd 3: Sl st in first ch sp, **beg pc** *(see Special Stitches)* in same ch sp, ch 5, [**pc** *(see Special Stitches)* in next st, ch 5] around, join with sl st in top of beg pc.

Rnd 4: Ch 1, [7 sc in next ch-5 sp, ch 10, drop lp from hook, insert hook in first sc of 7-sc group, pull dropped lp through, (7 sc, ch 3, 7 sc) in ch-10 sp just made] around, join.

Rnd 5: Sl st in each of first 7 sts, sl st in next ch sp, ch 9 *(counts as first tr and ch-5 sp)*, tr in same ch sp, ch 5, [(tr, ch 5, tr) in next ch sp, ch 5] around, join with sl st in fourth ch of beg ch-9.

Rnd 6: Ch 1, 6 sc in each ch sp around, join. *(120 sc)*

Rnd 7: Ch 1, sc in first st, [ch 5, sk next 3 sts, sc in next st] around to last 3 sts, sk last 3 sts, join with ch 2, dc in beg sc. *(30 ch-5 sps)*

Rnd 8: Beg pc around joining dc, ch 5, [pc in next ch sp, ch 5] around, join with sl st in beg pc.

Rnd 9: Rep rnd 4.

Rnd 10: Sl st in each of first 7 sts, (sl st, ch 9, tr) in next ch sp, (tr, ch 5, tr) in each ch sp around, join with sl st in fourth ch of beg ch-9.

Rnd 11: Ch 1, [7 sc in next ch sp, ch 1, (4 sc, ch 3, 4 sc) in next ch sp, ch 5, **turn**, (tr, ch 5, tr) in ch-3 sp, ch 5, sl st in next ch-1 sp, **turn**, (3 sc, ch 3, 3 sc) in each of next 3 ch-5 sps] around, join with sl st in beg sc. Fasten off.

Rnd 12: With RS facing, join with sc in center ch-3 sp of any point, *ch 10, **tr dec** *(see Special Stitches)* in next 2 ch-3 sps**, ch 10, sc in next ch sp, rep from * around, ending last rep at **, join with ch 5, dtr in beg sc.

Rnd 13: Ch 8 *(counts as beg dc and ch-5 sp)*, dc around joining dtr, ch 5, [(dc, ch 5, dc) in next ch-10 sp, ch 5] around, join with sl st in third ch of beg ch-8.

Rnd 14: Beg shell *(see Special Stitches)*, ch 5, sk next ch-5 sp, [**shell** *(see Special Stitches)* in next ch sp, ch 5, sk next ch sp] around, join with sl st in top of beg shell.

Rnds 15–17: Beg shell, ch 6, sk next ch sp, [shell in ch sp of

24 A Passion For Pineapples • Annie's Attic, Berne, IN 46711 • AnniesAttic.com

next shell, ch 6, sk next ch sp] around, join.

Rnd 18: Beg shell, ch 7, sk next ch sp, [shell in next shell, ch 7, sk next ch sp] around, join.

Rnd 19: Beg shell, ch 8, sk next ch sp, [shell in next shell, ch 8, sk next ch sp] around, join.

Rnd 20: Beg shell, ch 9, sk next ch sp, [shell in next shell, ch 9, sk next ch sp] around, join.

Rnd 21: Beg shell, ch 10, sk next ch sp, [shell in next shell, ch 10, sk next ch sp] around, join.

Rnd 22: Beg shell, ch 11, sk next ch sp, [shell in next shell, ch 11, sk next ch sp] around, join.

Rnd 23: Beg shell, ch 12, sk next ch sp, [shell in next shell, ch 12, sk next ch sp] around, join.

Rnd 24: Beg shell, ch 13, sk next ch sp, [shell in next shell, ch 13, sk next ch sp] around, join.

Rnd 25: Beg shell, ch 13, sk next ch sp, (pc, ch 10, pc) in next shell, ch 13, sk next ch sp] around, join.

Rnd 26: Beg shell, *ch 6, sk next ch-13 sp, 17 tr in next ch-10 sp, ch 6, sk next ch-13**, shell in next shell, rep from * around, ending last rep at **, join.

Rnd 27: Beg shell, *ch 5, [tr in next tr, ch 1] 16 times, tr in next tr, ch 5**, shell in next shell, rep from * around ending last rep at **, join.

Rnd 28: Beg shell, *ch 5, sk next ch-5 sp, [sc in next ch-1 sp, ch 3] 15 times, sc in next ch-1 sp, ch 5**, shell in next shell, rep from * around, ending last rep at **, join.

Rnd 29: Beg shell, *ch 5, sk next ch-5 sp, [pc in next ch-3 sp, ch 2] 14 times, pc in next ch-3 sp, ch 5**, shell in next shell, rep from * around, ending last rep at **, join.

Rnd 30: Beg shell, *ch 5, sk next ch-5 sp, [sc in next ch-2 sp, ch 3] 13 times, sc in next ch-2 sp, ch 5**, shell in next shell, rep from * around, ending last rep at **, join.

Rnd 31: Beg shell *ch 5, sk next ch-5 sp, [pc in next ch-3 sp, ch 2] 12 times, pc in next ch-3 sp, ch 5**, shell in next shell, rep from * around, ending last rep at **, join.

Rnd 32: Beg shell, *ch 5, sk next ch-5 sp, [sc in next ch-2 sp, ch 3] 11 times, sc in next ch-2 sp, ch 5**, shell in next shell, rep from * around, ending last rep at **, join.

Rnd 33: Sl st in next ch sp, (beg pc, ch 5, sc, ch 5, pc) in same ch sp, *ch 5, sk next ch sp, [pc in next ch-3 sp, ch 2] 10 times, pc in next ch-3 sp, ch 5**, (pc, ch 5, sc, ch 5, pc) in next shell, rep from * around, ending last rep at **, join with sl st in top of beg pc.

Rnd 34: Beg shell, *ch 5, shell in next ch sp, ch 5, sk next ch sp, [sc in next ch-2 sp, ch 3] 9 times, sc in next ch-2 sp, ch 5, sk next ch sp**, shell in next ch-sp, rep from * around, ending lat rep at **, join.

Rnd 35: Beg shell, *ch 5, sc in next ch sp, ch 5, shell in next shell, ch 5, sk next ch sp, [pc in next ch-3 sp, ch 2] 8 times, pc in next ch-3 sp, ch 5**, shell in next shell, rep from * around, ending last rep at **, join.

Rnd 36: Beg shell, *ch 5, sc in next ch sp, ch 10, sc in next ch sp, ch 5, shell in next shell, ch 5, sk next ch sp, [sc in next ch-2 sp, ch 3] 7 times, sc in next ch-2 sp, ch 5**, shell in next shell, rep from * around, ending last rep at **, join.

Rnd 37: Beg shell, *ch 1, sk next ch sp, 16 tr in next ch-10 sp, ch 1, shell in next shell, ch 5, sk next ch sp, [pc in next ch-3 sp, ch 2] 6 times, pc in next ch-3 sp, ch 5**, shell in next shell, rep from * around, ending last rep at **, join.

Rnd 38: Beg shell, *[ch 2, tr in each of next 2 tr] 8 times, ch 2, shell in next shell, ch 5, sk next ch sp, [sc in next ch-2 sp, ch 3] 5 times, sc in next ch-2 sp, ch 5**, shell in next shell, rep from * around, ending last rep at **, join.

Rnd 39: Beg shell, *[ch 3, tr in each of next 2 tr] 8 times, ch 3, shell in next shell, ch 5, sk next ch sp, [pc in next ch-3 sp, ch 2] 4 times, pc in next ch-3 sp, ch 5**, shell in next shell, rep from * around, ending last rep at **, join.

Rnd 40: Beg shell, *[ch 4, tr in each of next 2 tr] 8 times, ch 4, shell in next shell, ch 5, sk next ch sp, [sc in next ch-2 sp, ch 3] 3 times, sc in next ch-2 sp, ch 5**, shell in next shell, rep from * around, ending last rep at **, join.

Rnd 41: Beg shell, *[ch 5, tr in each of next 2 tr] 8 times, ch 5, shell in next shell, ch 5, sk next ch sp, [pc in next ch-3 sp, ch 2] twice, pc in next ch-3 sp, ch 5**, shell in next shell, rep from * around, ending last rep at **, join.

Rnd 42: Beg shell, *ch 12, 2 tr in next ch-5 sp, tr in each of next 2 tr, 2 tr in next ch-5 sp, ch 12, [2 tr in same ch sp as last tr, tr in each of next 2 tr, 2 tr in next ch-5 sp, ch 12] 7 times, shell in next shell, ch 5, sk next ch sp, sc in next ch-2 sp, ch 3, sc in next ch-2 sp, ch 5**, shell in next shell, rep from * around, ending last rep at **, join.

Rnd 43: (Sl st, ch 1, sc) in first ch sp, *(3 sc {ch 3, 3 sc} 4 times) in next ch-12 sp, [sk next tr, tr dec in next 4 sts, sk next tr, (3 sc {ch 3, 3 sc} 4 times) in next ch-12 sp] 8 times, sc in next shell, sk next ch sp, tr in next ch-3 sp**, sc in next shell, rep from * around, ending last rep at **, join with sl st in beg sc. Fasten off.

NAPKIN
Note: Roll a narrow hem around linen square

Rnd 1: Join with sc ¼ inch before any corner, 2 sc across edge, 5 sc in corner, sc around edge *(in multiples of 8 dc plus 3)* with 5 sc in each corner, join with sl st in beg sc.

Rnd 2: Ch 1, sc in each of first 3 sts, *[ch 10, sk next 5 sts, sc in each of next 3 sts] across to next corner, rep from * around to last 5 sts, ch 10, sk last 5 sts, join with sl st in beg sc.

Rnd 3: (Sl st, ch 1, sc) in next st, (3 sc, {ch 3, 3 sc} 4 times) in next ch sp, [sk next sc, sc in next sc, (3 sc, {ch 3, 3 sc} 4 times) in next ch sp] around, join. Fasten off.

Pineapples in the Round

Design by Jo Ann Maxwell

SKILL LEVEL
■■■□ INTERMEDIATE

FINISHED SIZE
43 inches in diameter

MATERIALS
- J. & P. Coats South Maid crochet cotton size 10 (350 yds per ball):
    4 balls #42 cream
- Size 5/1.90mm steel crochet hook or size needed to obtain gauge

GAUGE
First 3 rnds = 2½ inches in diameter

SPECIAL STITCHES
Beginning shell (beg shell): Ch 3 *(counts as first dc)*, (dc, ch 2, 2 dc) in same ch sp.
Shell: (2 dc, ch 2, 2 dc) in indicated ch sp.
Picot: Ch 3, sl st in last sc made.
Beginning double shell (beg dbl shell): (Beg shell, ch 2, 2 dc) in indicated ch sp.
Double shell (dbl shell): (Shell, ch 2, 2 dc) in indicated ch sp.

INSTRUCTIONS
TABLECLOTH
Rnd 1: Ch 4, sl st in first ch to form a ring, ch 3 *(counts as first dc throughout)*, 19 dc in ring, join with sl st in third ch of beg ch-3. *(20 dc)*

Rnd 2: Ch 4 *(counts as first tr)*, tr in same st, ch 3, [sk next st, 2 tr in next st, ch 3] around, join with sl st in fourth ch of beg ch-4.

Rnd 3: Ch 3, dc in same st, ch 2, 2 dc in next tr, *ch 1, sc in next ch sp, ch 1**, 2 dc in next tr, ch 2, 2 dc in next tr, rep from * around, ending last rep at **, join with sl st in third ch of beg ch-3.

Rnd 4: Sl st in next dc and in ch-2 sp, **beg shell** *(see Special Stitches)* in same ch sp, ch 5, [**shell** *(see Special Stitches)* in next ch-2 sp, ch 5] around, join. *(10 shells)*

Rnd 5: Sl st in next dc and in ch-2 sp, beg shell in same ch sp, *ch 3, sc in next ch-5 sp, ch 3**, shell in next shell, rep from * around, ending last rep at **, join.

Rnd 6: Sl st in next dc and in ch-2 sp, ch 3, 8 dc in same ch sp, *sc in next ch-3 sp, ch 5, sc in next ch-3 sp**, 9 dc in next shell, rep from * around, ending last rep at **, join.

Rnd 7: Sl st in each of next 4 dc, ch 10 *(counts as first dc, ch-7)*, *(sc, **picot**—see Special Stitches) in next ch-5 sp, ch 7**, dc in fifth dc of next 9-dc group, ch 7, rep from * around, ending last rep at **, join with sl st in third ch of beg ch-10.

Rnd 8: Beg shell in same st as joining, *ch 2, sc in next ch-7 sp, ch 7, sc in next ch-7 sp, ch 2**, shell in next dc, rep from * around, ending last rep at **, join.

Rnd 9: Sl st in next dc and in ch-2 sp, beg shell in same ch sp, *ch 5, shell in fourth ch of next ch-7, ch 5**, shell in next shell sp, rep from * around, ending last rep at **, join.

Rnd 10: Sl st in next dc and in ch-2 sp, beg shell in same ch sp, *ch 2, sc in next ch-5 sp, dc in ch sp of next shell, (ch 1, dc) 7 times in same ch sp, sc in next ch-5 sp, ch 2**, shell in ch sp of next shell, rep from * around, ending last rep at **, join.

Rnd 11: Sl st in next dc and in ch-2 sp, **beg dbl shell** *(see Special Stitches)* in same ch sp, *ch 3, sk next ch-2 sp, [sc in next dc, ch 3] 8 times**, **dbl shell** *(see Special Stitches)* in next shell, rep from * around, ending last rep at **, join.

Rnd 12: Sl st in next dc and in ch-2 sp, beg shell in same ch sp, *ch 1, shell in next ch-2 sp, ch 3, sk next ch-3 sp, [sc in next ch-3 sp,

26 A Passion For Pineapples • Annie's Attic, Berne, IN 46711 • AnniesAttic.com

ch 3] 7 times**, shell in next ch-2 sp, rep from * around, ending last rep at **, join.

Rnd 13: Sl st in next dc and in ch-2 sp, beg shell in same ch sp, *ch 2, shell in next shell, ch 3, sk next ch-3 sp, [sc in next ch-3 sp, ch 3] 6 times**, shell in next shell, rep from * around, ending last rep at **, join.

Rnd 14: Sl st in next dc and in ch-2 sp, beg shell in same ch sp, *ch 3, shell in next shell, ch 3, sk next ch-3 sp, [sc in next ch-3 sp, ch 3] 5 times**, shell in next shell, rep from * around, ending last rep at **, join.

Rnd 15: Sl st in next dc and in ch-2 sp, beg shell in same ch sp, *ch 3, sc in next ch-3 sp, ch 3, shell in next shell, ch 3, sk next ch-3 sp, [sc in next ch-3 sp, ch 3] 4 times**, shell in next shell, rep from * around, ending last rep at **, join.

Rnd 16: Sl st in next dc and in ch-2 sp, beg shell in same ch sp, *ch 3, sc in next ch-3 sp, ch 5, sc in next ch-3 sp, ch 3, shell in next shell, ch 3, sk next ch-3 sp, [sc in next ch-3 sp, ch 3] 3 times**, shell in next shell, rep from * around, ending last rep at **, join.

Rnd 17: Sl st in next dc and in ch-2 sp, beg shell in same ch sp, *ch 3, sc in next ch-3 sp, ch 5, sk first ch of next ch-5 sp, dc in each of next 3 chs, ch 5, sc in next ch-3 sp, ch 3, shell in next shell, ch 3, sk next ch-3 sp, [sc in next ch-3 sp, ch 3] twice**, shell in next shell, rep from * around, ending last rep at **, join.

Rnd 18: Sl st in next dc and in ch-2 sp, beg shell in same ch sp, *sc in next ch-3 sp, ch 5, dc in each of last 3 chs of next ch-5 sp, ch 5, sk 3 dc, dc in each of first 3 chs of next ch-5 sp, ch 5, sc in next ch-3 sp, ch 3, shell in next shell, ch 3, sk next ch-3 sp, sc in next ch-3 sp, ch 3**, shell in next shell, rep from * around, ending last rep at **, join.

Rnd 19: Sl st in next dc and in ch-2 sp, beg shell in same sp, *ch 3, sc in next ch-3 sp, ch 5, dc in each of last 3 chs of next ch-5 sp, ch 5, sc in next ch-5 sp, ch 5, sk next 3 dc, dc in each of first 3 chs of next ch-5 sp, ch 5, sc in next ch-3 sp, ch 3**, shell in each of next 2 shells rep from * around, ending last rep at **, shell in last shell join.

Rnd 20: Sl st in next dc and in ch-2 sp, ch 1, sc in same ch sp, *ch 5, sc in next ch-3 sp, ch 5, dc in each of last 3 chs of next ch-5 sp, ch 5, sc in fifth ch of next ch-5 sp, sc in next sc, sc in first ch of next ch-5 sp, ch 5, sk next 3 dc, dc in each of first 3 chs of next ch-5 sp, ch 5, sc in next ch-3 sp**, [ch 5, sc in ch sp of next shell] twice, rep from * around, ending last rep at **, ch 5, sc in ch sp of last shell, ch 5, join with sl st in beg sc.

Rnd 21: Sl st in each of next 3 chs, ch 1, sc in same ch sp, *ch 5, dc in each of last 3 chs of next ch-5 sp, ch 5, sc in last ch of next ch-5 sp, sc in each of next 3 sc, sc in first ch of next ch-5 sp, ch 5, sk next 3 dc, dc in each of first 3 chs of next ch-5 sp, ch 5, sc in next ch-5 sp, ch 5, (sc, ch 5) 4 times in next ch-5 sp**, sc in next ch-5 sp, rep from * around, ending last rep at **, join.

Rnd 22: Sl st in each of next 3 chs, ch 1, sc in same ch sp, *ch 5, dc in each of first 3 chs of next ch-5 sp, ch 5, sk next sc, sc in each of next 3 sc, ch 5, dc in each of last 3 chs of next ch-5 sp, ch 5, [sc in next ch-5 sp, ch 5] 6 times**, sc in next ch-5 sp, rep from * around, ending last rep at **, join.

Rnd 23: Sl st in each of next 3 chs, ch 1, sc in same ch sp, *ch 5, dc in each of first 3 chs of next ch-5 sp, ch 5, sk next sc, sc in next sc, ch 5, dc in each of last 3 chs of next ch-5 sp, ch 5, [sc in next ch-5 sp, ch 5] 7 times**, sc in next ch-5 sp, rep from * around, ending last rep at **, join.

Rnd 24: Sl st in each of next 3 chs, ch 1, sc in same ch sp, *ch 5, dc in each of first 3 chs of next ch-5 sp, ch 3, dc in each of last 3 chs of next ch-5 sp, ch 5, [sc in next ch-5 sp, ch 5] 8 times**, sc in next ch-5 sp, rep from * around, ending last rep at **, join.

Rnd 25: Sl st in each of next 3 chs, ch 1, sc in same ch sp, *ch 5, sk next 3 dc, dc in each of next 3 chs, ch 5, [sc in next ch-5 sp, ch 5] 9 times**, sc in next ch-5 sp, rep from * around, ending last rep at **, join.

Rnd 26: Sl st in each of next 3 chs, ch 1, sc in same ch sp, ch 5, [sc in next ch-5 sp, ch 5] 5 times, *sk first ch of next ch-5 sp, dc in each of next 3 chs**, ch 5, [sc in next ch-5 sp, ch 5] 10 times, rep from * around, ending last rep at **, ch 5, [sc in next ch-5 sp, ch 5] 4 times, join.

Rnd 27: Sl st in next ch-5 sp, ch 1, (sc, ch 5) 4 times in same ch sp, *[sc in next ch-5 sp, ch 5] 4 times, dc in each of last 3 chs of next ch-5 sp, ch 5, sk next 3 dc, dc in each of first 3 chs of next ch-5 sp, ch 5, [sc in next ch-5 sp, ch 5] 4 times**, (sc, ch 5) 4 times in next ch-5 sp, rep from * around, ending last rep at **, join.

Rnd 28: Sl st in each of next 3 chs, ch 1, sc in same ch sp, ch 5, [sc in next ch-5 sp, ch 5] 6 times, *dc in each of last 3 chs of next ch-5 sp, ch 5, sc in next ch-5 sp, ch 5, dc in each of first 3 chs of next ch-5 sp, ch 5**, [sc in next ch-5 sp, ch 5] 11 times, rep from * around, ending last rep at **, [sc in next ch-5 sp, ch 5] 4 times, join.

Rnd 29: Sl st in each of next 3 chs, ch 1, sc in same ch sp, ch 5, [sc in next ch-5 sp, ch 5] 5 times, *dc in each of last 3 chs of next ch-5 sp, ch 5, sc in last ch of next ch-5 sp, sc in next sc, sc in next ch, ch 5, sk next 3 dc, dc in each of first 3 chs of next ch-5 sp, ch 5**, [sc in next ch-5 sp, ch 5] 10 times, rep from * around, ending last rep at **, [sc in next ch-5 sp, ch 5] 3 times, sc in next ch-5 sp, ch 2, dc in beg sc to form last ch-5 sp.

Rnd 30: Beg shell in sp just formed, *[ch 3, shell in next ch-5 sp] twice, ch 3, [sc in next ch-5 sp, ch 5] 3 times, dc in each of last 3 chs of next ch-5 sp, ch 5, sc in last ch of next ch-5 sp, sc in each of next 3 sc, sc in next ch, ch 5, sk next 3 dc, dc in each of first 3 chs of next ch-5 sp, [ch 5, sc in next ch-5 sp] 3 times, ch 3**, shell in next ch-5 sp, rep from * around, ending last rep at **, join in third ch of beg ch-3.

Rnd 31: Sl st in next dc and in ch-2 sp, beg shell in same ch sp, *ch 3, sc in next ch-3 sp, 8 dc in ch sp of next shell, sc in next ch-3 sp, ch 3, shell in next shell, ch 3, [sc in next ch-5 sp, ch 5] 3 times, sk next 3 dc, dc in each of first 3 chs of next ch-5 sp, ch 5, sk next sc, sc in each of next 3 sc, ch 5, dc in each of last 3 chs of next ch-5 sp, [ch 5, sc in next ch-5 sp] 3 times, ch 3**, shell in next shell, rep from * around, ending last rep at **, join

Rnd 32: Sl st in next dc and in ch-2 sp, beg shell in same ch sp, *ch 3, sk next ch-3 sp, [sc in next dc, ch 3] 8 times, shell in next shell, ch 3, sk next ch-3 sp, [sc in next ch-5 sp, ch 5] 3 times, sk next 3 dc, dc in each of first 3 chs of next ch-5 sp, ch 5, sk next sc, sc in next sc, ch 5, dc in each of last 3 chs of next ch-5 sp, [ch 5, sc in next ch-5 sp] 3 times, ch 3**, shell in next shell, rep from * around, ending last rep at **, join.

Rnd 33: Sl st in next dc and in ch-2 sp, beg shell in same ch sp, *ch 3, sk next ch-3 sp, [sc in next ch-3 sp, ch 3] 7 times, shell in next shell, ch 5, sk next ch-3 sp, [sc in next ch-5 sp, ch 5] 3 times, sk next 3 dc, dc in each of first 3 chs of next ch-5 sp, ch 3, dc in each of last 3 chs of next ch-5 sp, ch 5, [sc in next ch-5 sp, ch 5] 3 times**, shell in next shell, rep from * around, ending last rep at **, join.

Rnd 34: Sl st in next dc and in ch-2 sp, beg shell in same ch sp, *ch 3, sk next ch-3 sp, [sc in next ch-3 sp, ch 3] 6 times, shell in next shell, ch 5, [sc in next ch-5 sp, ch 5] 4 times, sk next 3 dc, dc in each of next 3 chs, ch 5, [sc in next ch-5 sp, ch 5] 4 times**, shell in next shell, rep from * around, ending last rep at **, join.

Rnd 35: Sl st in next dc and in ch-2 sp, beg shell in same ch sp, *ch 3, sk next ch-3 sp, [sc in next ch-3 sp, ch 3] 5 times, shell in next shell sp, ch 5, [sc in next ch-5 sp, ch 5] 10 times**, shell in next shell, rep from * around, ending last rep at **, join.

Rnd 36: Sl st in next dc and in ch-2 sp, beg shell in same ch sp, *ch 3, sk next ch-3 sp, [sc in next ch-3 sp, ch 3] 4 times, shell in next shell, ch 5, [sc in next ch-5 sp, ch 5] 5 times, (sc, ch 5) 3 times in next ch-5 sp, [sc in next ch-5 sp, ch 5] 5 times**, shell in next shell sp, rep from * around, ending last rep at **, join.

Rnd 37: Sl st in next dc and in ch-2 sp, beg shell in same ch sp, *ch 3, sk next ch-3 sp, [sc in next ch-3 sp, ch 3] 3 times, shell in next shell, ch 5, [sc in next ch-5 sp, ch 5] 14 times**, shell in next shell, rep from * around, ending last rep at **, join.

Rnd 38: Sl st in next dc and in ch-2 sp, beg shell in same ch sp, *ch 3, sk next ch-3 sp, [sc in next ch-3 sp, ch 3] twice, shell in next shell, ch 5, [sc in next ch-5 sp, ch 5] 15 times**, shell in next shell, rep from * around, ending last rep at **, join.

Rnd 39: Sl st in next dc and in ch-2 sp, beg shell in same ch sp, *ch 3, sk next ch-3 sp, sc in next ch-3 sp, ch 3, shell in next shell, ch 5, [sc in next ch-5 sp, ch 5] 16 times**, shell in next shell, rep from * around, ending last rep at **, join.

Rnd 40: Sl st in next dc and in ch-2 sp, beg shell in same ch sp, shell in next shell, *ch 5, [sc in next ch-5 sp, ch 5] 17 times**, shell in each of next 2 shells, rep from * around, ending last rep at **, join.

Rnd 41: Sl st in next dc and in ch-2 sp, ch 1, sc in same ch sp, ch 5, sc in next shell, ch 5, *[sc in next ch-5 sp, ch 5] 18 times**, [sc in next shell, ch 5] twice, rep from * around, ending last rep at **, join.

Rnds 42 & 43: Sl st in each of next 3 chs, ch 1, sc in same ch sp, ch 5, [sc in next ch-5 sp, ch 5] around, join with sl st in beg sc.

Rnd 44: Sl st in each of next 3 chs, ch 1, sc in same ch sp, *[ch 5, sc in next ch-5 sp] 8 times, ch 3, dbl shell in next ch-5 sp, ch 3**, sc in next ch-5 sp, rep from * around, ending last rep at **, join.

Rnd 45: Sl st in each of next 3 chs, ch 1, sc in same sp, *[ch 5, sc in next ch-5 sp] 7 times, [ch 3, shell in next ch-2 sp] twice, ch 3**, sc in next ch-5 sp, rep from * around, ending last rep at **, join.

Rnd 46: Sl st in each of next 3 chs, ch 1, sc in same ch sp, *[ch 5, sc in next ch-5 sp] 6 times, ch 3, shell in next shell, ch 3, (sc, picot) in next ch-3 sp, ch 3, shell in next shell, ch 3**, sc in next ch-5 sp, rep from * around, ending last rep at **, join.

Rnd 47: Sl st in each of next 3 chs, ch 1, sc in same ch sp, *[ch 5, sc in next ch-5 sp] 5 times, ch 3, shell in next shell, ch 3, sc in next ch-3 sp, ch 5, sc in next ch-3 sp, ch 3, shell in next shell sp, ch 3**, sc in next ch-5 sp, rep from* around, ending last rep at **, join.

Rnd 48: Sl st in each of next 3 chs, ch 1, sc in same ch sp, *[ch 5, sc in next ch-5 sp] 4 times, ch 3, shell in next shell, ch 3, sk next ch-3 sp, 14 dc in next ch-5 sp, ch 3, shell in next shell, ch 3**, sc in next ch-5 sp, rep from * around, ending last rep at **, join.

Rnd 49: Sl st in each of next 3 chs, ch 1, sc in same ch sp, *[ch 5, sc in next ch-5 sp] 3 times, ch 3, shell in next shell, ch 3, sc in next ch-3 sp, dc in next dc, [ch 1, dc in next dc] 13 times, sc in next ch-3 sp, ch 3, shell in next shell, ch 3**, sc in next ch-5 sp, rep from * around, ending last rep at **, join.

Rnd 50: Sl st in each of next 3 chs, ch 1, sc in same ch sp, *[ch 5, sc in next ch-5 sp] twice, ch 3, dbl shell in next shell, ch 3, sk next ch-3 sp, [sc in next dc, ch 3] 14 times, dbl shell in next shell, ch 3**, sc in next ch-5 sp, rep from * around, ending last rep at **, join.

Rnd 51: Sl st in each of next 3 chs, ch 1, sc in same ch sp, *ch

5, sc in next ch-5 sp, [ch 3, shell in next ch-2 sp] twice, ch 3, sk next ch-3 sp, [sc in next ch-3 sp, ch 3] 13 times, [shell in next ch-2 sp, ch 3] twice**, sc in next ch-5 sp, rep from * around, ending last rep at **, join.

Rnd 52: Sl st in each of next 3 chs, ch 1, sc in same ch sp, *ch 3, **shell in next shell, ch 3, sc in next ch-3 sp, ch 3, shell in next shell, ch 3, sk next ch-3 sp**, [sc in next ch-3 sp, ch 3] 12 times, rep from ** to **, sc in next ch-3 sp, rep from * around, join.

Rnd 53: Sl st in each of next 3 chs, in each of next 2 dc and in next ch-2 sp, ch 1, sc in same ch sp, *ch 4, [sc in next ch-3 sp, ch 4] twice**, shell in next shell, ch 3, sk next ch-3 sp, [sc in next ch-3 sp, ch 3] 11 times, shell in next shell, rep from * to **, [sc in ch sp of next shell] twice, rep from * around, ending with sc in ch sp of last shell, join.

Rnd 54: Sl st in each of next 2 chs, ch 4 *(counts as first dc, ch-1)*, *[sc in next ch-4 sp, ch 4] twice, shell in next shell, ch 3, sk next ch-3 sp, [sc in next ch-3 sp, ch 3] 10 times, shell in next shell, [ch 4, sc in next ch-4 sp] twice, ch 1, dc in next ch-4 sp, ch 3**, dc in next ch-4 sp, ch 1, rep from * around, ending last rep at **, join with sl st in third ch of beg ch-4.

Rnd 55: Sl st in next ch, in next sc, and in each of next 2 chs, ch 1, sc in same ch sp, *ch 4, sc in next ch-4 sp, ch 4, shell in next shell, ch 3, sk next ch-3 sp, [sc in next ch-3 sp, ch 3] 9 times, shell in next shell, [ch 4, sc in next ch-4 sp] twice, ch 1 (tr, ch 3, tr) in next ch-3 sp, ch 1**, sc in next ch-4 sp, rep from * around, ending last rep at **, join.

Rnd 56: Sc in each of next 2 chs, ch 1, sc in same ch sp, *ch 4, (sc, picot) in next ch-4 sp, ch 4, shell in next shell, ch 3, sk next ch-3 sp, [sc in next ch-3 sp, ch 3] 8 times, shell in next shell, ch 4, (sc, picot) in next ch-4 sp, ch 4, sc in next ch-4 sp, 7 dc in next ch-3 sp**, sc in next ch-4 sp, rep from * around, ending last rep at **, join. Fasten off.

FIRST PINEAPPLE
Row 57: Join thread with sl st in ch sp of next unworked shell of rnd 56, beg shell in same ch sp, ch 3, sk next ch-3 sp, [sc in next ch-3 sp, ch 3] 7 times, shell in next shell leaving rem sts unworked, turn.

Row 58: Ch 3, shell in first shell, ch 3, sk next ch-3 sp, [sc in next ch-3 sp, ch 3] 6 times, shell in next shell, turn.

Row 59: Ch 3, shell in first shell, ch 3, sk next ch-3 sp, [sc in next ch-3 sp, ch 3] 5 times, shell in next shell, turn.

Row 60: Ch 3, shell in first shell, ch 3, sk next ch-3 sp, [sc in next ch-3 sp, ch 3] 4 times, shell in next shell, turn.

Row 61: Ch 3, shell in first shell, ch 3, sk next ch-3 sp, [sc in next ch-3 sp, ch 3] 3 times, shell in next shell, turn.

Row 62: Ch 3, shell in first shell, ch 3, sk next ch-3 sp, [sc in next ch-3 sp, ch 3] twice, shell in next shell, turn.

Row 63: Ch 3, shell in first shell, ch 3, sk next ch-3 sp, sc in next ch-3 sp, ch 3, shell in next shell, turn.

Row 64: Ch 3, [shell in next shell] twice. Fasten off.

Rep rows 57–64 for each of rem 19 Pineapples.

Pineapple Rose Afghan

Design by Jo Ann Maxwell

SKILL LEVEL
■■■□ INTERMEDIATE

FINISHED SIZE
72 inches long x 54 inches wide

MATERIALS
- Red Heart Super Saver medium (worsted) weight yarn (8 oz/452 yds/226g per skein):
    6 skeins #313 aran
- Size J/10/6mm crochet hook or size needed to obtain gauge

GAUGE
First 5 rnds of Motif = 4½ inches in diameter

PATTERN NOTES
Referring to joining diagram, make and join a total of six Motifs for center strip, leaving six chain-6 spaces free on each side of joined section.

Make and join five Motifs on each side of center strip for inner strips, joining as many adjacent sides as necessary in same manner as for Second Motif.

Make and join four Motifs to each outside edge of each inner strip for outer strips. There will be 102 free chain-6 spaces around outside edge when last Motif is joined.

SPECIAL STITCHES
Beginning shell (beg shell): (Ch 3—*counts as first dc*, dc, ch 2, 2 dc) in indicated ch sp.
Shell: (2 dc, ch 2, 2 dc) in indicated ch sp.

INSTRUCTIONS
FIRST MOTIF
Rnd 1: Ch 4, sl st in first ch to form ring, ch 1, 9 sc in ring, join with sl st in beg sc. *(9 sc)*
Rnd 2: Ch 1, sc in first st, ch 2, [sc in next sc, ch 2] around, join. *(9 ch-2 sps)*
Rnd 3: Ch 1, (sc, 4 dc, sc) in each

ch-2 sp around, join in beg sc of rnd 2. *(9 petals)*
Rnd 4: Ch 1, sc in first st, ch 3, [working from behind rnd 3 petals, sc in next rnd 2 sc, ch 3] around, join. *(9 ch-3 sps)*
Rnd 5: Ch 1, (sc, 5 dc, sc) in each ch-3 sp around, join with sl st in beg sc of rnd 4. *(9 petals)*
Rnd 6: Ch 1, sc in first st, ch 5, [working behind rnd 5 petals, sc in next rnd 4 sc, ch 5] around, join in beg sc. *(9 ch-5 sps)*
Rnd 7: Sl st in next ch-5 sp, ch 3 *(counts as first dc)*, (2 dc, ch 2, 3 dc) in same ch sp, (3 dc, ch 2, 3 dc) in each ch-5 sp around, join with sl st in third ch of beg ch-3.
Rnd 8: Sl st back in sp between last dc just made and beg ch-3 of rnd 7, ch 1, sc in same sp, *ch 5, sc in next ch-2 sp, ch 5**, sk next 3 dc, sc in sp before next dc, rep from * around, ending last rep at **, join with sl st in beg sc. *(18 ch-5 sps)*
Rnd 9: Sl st in each of next 3 chs, ch 1, sc in same ch sp, ch 6, [sc in next ch-5 sp, ch 6] around, join. Fasten off. *(18 ch-6 sps)*

SECOND & REMAINING MOTIFS
Make 23.

Rnds 1–8: Rep rnds 1–8 of First Motif.

JOINING
Rnd 9: Sl st in each of next 3 chs, ch 1, sc in same ch sp, ch 3, sl st in ch-6 sp on previous Motif, ch 3, sc in next ch-5 sp on working motif, [ch 3, sl st in next ch-6 sp on previous Motif, ch 3, sc in next ch-5 sp on working motif] twice *(3 ch-6 sps; one adjacent side joined, see Pattern notes)*, complete rnd as for First Motif. Fasten off.

PINEAPPLE BORDER
Rnd 1: With RS facing, join with sl st in ch-6 sp indicated on illustration, ch 1, sc in same ch sp, working in free ch-6 sps around, *[ch 6, sc in next ch-6 sp] 17 times, ch 3, [**shell** *(see Special Stitches)* in next ch-6 sp, ch 2] twice, shell in next ch-6 sp, ch 3, **sc in next ch-6 sp, [ch 6, sc in next ch-6 sp] 11 times, ch 3, [shell in next ch-6 sp, ch 2] twice, shell in next ch-6 sp, ch 3**, rep between **, sc in next ch-6 sp, rep from * around, join with sl st in beg sc.

Rnd 2: Sl st in each of next 3 chs, ch 1, sc in same sp, ◊*ch 3, [shell in next ch-6 sp, ch 2] twice, shell in next ch-6 sp, ch 3, sc in next ch-6 sp**, [ch 6, sc in next ch-6 sp] twice*, rep between *, rep from * to **, {ch 6, shell in next shell, ch 3, sc in next ch-2 sp, dc in next shell sp, (ch 1, dc) 7 times in same ch sp, sc in next ch-2 sp, ch 3, shell in next shell, ch 6, sc in next ch-6 sp}, [rep between *, rep from * to **, rep between { }] twice, rep from ◊ around, join.

Rnd 3: Sl st in each of next 3 chs, in each of next 2 dc and in next ch-2 sp, **beg shell** *(see Special Stitches)* in same ch sp, ◊*ch 3, sc in next ch-2 sp, dc in next shell, (ch 1, dc) 6 times in same ch sp, sc in next ch-2 sp, ch 3, shell in next shell, ch 3, sc in next ch-6 sp, ch 6**, sc in next ch-6 sp, ch 3, shell in next shell *, rep between *, rep from * to **, {shell in next shell, ch 3, sk next ch-3 sp, [sc in next dc, ch 3] 8 times, shell in next shell, ch 6, sc in next ch-6 sp, ch 3, shell in next shell sp}, [rep from * to *, rep from * to **, rep between { }] twice, rep from ◊ around, join with sl st in third ch of beg ch-3.

Rnd 4: Sl st in next dc and in ch-2 sp, beg shell in same ch sp, *ch 3, sk next ch-3 sp, [sc in next dc, ch 3] 7 times, shell in next shell, ch 6, sc in next ch-6 sp, ch 6, shell in next shell*, **rep between * twice, ch 3, sk next ch-3 sp, [sc in next ch-3 sp, ch 3] 7 times, shell in next shell, ch 6, sc in next ch-6 sp, ch 6, shell in next shell, rep from ** twice, rep from * around, join.

Rnd 5: Sl st in next dc and in ch-2 sp, beg shell in same ch sp, *ch 3, sk next ch-3 sp, [sc in next ch-3 sp, ch 3] 6 times, shell in next shell, ch 3, sc in next ch-6 sp, ch 6, sc in next ch-6 sp, ch 3, shell in next shell, rep from * around, join.

FIRST PINEAPPLE
Row 6: Sl st in next dc and in ch-2 sp, beg shell in same ch sp, ch 3, sk next ch-3 sp, [sc in next ch-3 sp, ch 3] 5 times, shell in next shell, turn.

Row 7: Ch 3, shell in first shell, ch 3, sk next ch-3 sp, [sc in next ch-3 sp, ch 3] 4 times, shell in next shell, turn.

Row 8: Ch 3, shell in first shell, ch 3, sk next ch-3 sp, [sc in next ch-3 sp, ch 3] 3 times, shell in next shell, turn.

Row 9: Ch 3, shell in first shell, ch 3, sk next ch-3 sp, [sc in next ch-3 sp, ch 3] twice, shell in next shell, turn.

Row 10: Ch 3, shell in first shell, ch 3, sk next ch-3 sp, [sc in next ch-3 sp, ch 3], shell in next shell, turn.

Row 11: Ch 3, shell in each of next 2 shells. Fasten off.

SECOND PINEAPPLE
Row 6: With RS facing, join with sl st in next unworked shell of rnd 5, beg shell in same ch sp, ch 3, sk next ch-3 sp, [sc in next ch-3 sp, ch 3] 5 times, shell in next shell, turn.

Rows 7–11: Rep rows 7–11 of First Pineapple, **do not fasten off** at end of last row, turn.

Rnd 12: Ch 1, sc in last dc made, *[ch 4, sc in ch sp of next shell] twice, working in ends of rows, [ch 4, sc in next beg ch-3, ch 4, sc in end dc of next row] 3 times, ch 4, sc in next ch-6 sp, beg with next row 6, [ch 4, sc in end st of next row] 6 times to top of pineapple, rep from * around, ending with [ch 4, sc in end st of next row] 5 times, ch 4, join.

Rnd 13: Sl st in each of next 2 chs, ch 1, sc in same ch sp, ◊*dc in next ch-4 sp, [(ch 1, dc) in same sp] 6 times, sc in next ch-4 sp, **dc in next ch-4 sp, ({ch 1, dc} 4 times) in same ch sp, sc in next ch sp**, rep between ** 3 times, sc in next ch-4 sp, rep from * to **, rep from ◊ around, join. Fasten off.

Next rows: Rep rows 6–13 of Second Pineapple for each of rem 18 Pineapples.

FINISHING
Wash Afghan; spin-dry. Spread Afghan on towels on flat surface. Shape each Flower; iron lightly over each Flower using damp pressing cloth for approximately two seconds; shape petals again. Let dry.❑❑

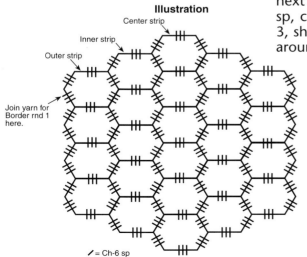

Illustration

Center strip
Inner strip
Outer strip

Join yarn for Border rnd 1 here.

╱ = Ch-6 sp

Pineapples for Baby

Design by Mary Layfield

SKILL LEVEL
■■■□ INTERMEDIATE

FINISHED SIZE
Infant's 6–12 months

FINISHED GARMENT MEASUREMENT
19½-inch chest

MATERIALS
- Fine (baby) weight yarn: 10 oz/1700 yds/284g pink
- Size D/3/3.25mm crochet hook or size needed to obtain gauge
- Sewing needle
- Embroidery needle
- 42 inches ⅛-inch-wide pink ribbon
- 5 pink 18mm ribbon roses
- 5 snaps
- Pink sewing thread
- 4 small pink buttons
- 5½-inch square flexible iron-on vinyl

GAUGE
14 sc = 2 inches, 3 sc rows and 2 cross st rows = 1 inch
Check gauge to save time.

SPECIAL STITCHES
Cross stitch (cross st): Sk next st, dc in next st, dc in sk st.
V-stitch (V-st): (Dc, ch 3, dc) in next ch sp on **Skirt** and (dc, ch 2, dc) on **Sleeves**.
Shell: (2 dc, ch 3, 2 dc) in next ch sp on **Skirt** and (2 dc, ch 2, 2 dc) in **Sleeves.**
Large shell (L-shell): (3 dc, ch 3, 3 dc) in next ch sp.

INSTRUCTIONS
DRESS
Bodice Front
Row 1 (RS): Ch 70, sc in second ch from hook and in each ch across, turn. *(69 sc)*
Row 2: Ch 3 *(counts as first dc)*, **cross st** *(see Special Stitches)* across, turn. *(69 sts—each cross st is counted as 2 dc)*
Row 3: Ch 1, sc in each st across, turn.
Rows 4 & 5: Rep rows 2 and 3.
Row 6: For **armhole**, ch 1, sc in each of first 4 sts, dc in each of next 2 sts, cross st across to last 7 sts, dc in each of next 2 sts, sc in next st leaving last 4 sts unworked for **armhole,** turn. *(65 sts)*
Row 7: Sl st in each of first 2 sts, sc in each st across leaving last 6 sts unworked, turn. *(59 sc)*
Row 8: Ch 3, dc in next st, cross st across to last sc, dc in last sc. leaving sl sts unworked, turn.
Row 9: Ch 1, sc in each st across leaving last st unworked, turn. *(56 sc)*
Row 10: Ch 3, cross st across to last 3 sts, dc in each of next 2 sts, leave last st unworked, turn. *(55 sts)*
Row 11: Ch 1, sc in each st across, turn. *(55 sc)*
Row 12: Ch 3, cross st across, turn.
Rows 13–20: Rep rows 11 and 12 alternately.
Row 21: Ch 1, 2 sc in first st, sc in each st across with 2 sc in last st, turn. *(57 sc)*
Row 22: For **first shoulder,** ch 3, cross st across next 18 sts, sc in each of next 2 sts leaving rem sts unworked, turn. *(21 sts)*
Row 23: Ch 1, sc in each st across, turn.
Row 24: Ch 3, cross st across next 16 sts, sc in next st leaving last 3 sts unworked, turn. *(18 sts)*
Row 25: Ch 1, sc in each st across, turn.
Row 26: Ch 1, sc in each of first 4 sts, dc in next st, cross st across next 12 sts leaving last st unworked, turn. *(17 sts)*
Row 27: Ch 1, sk first st, sc in each of next 9 sts leaving last 7 sts unworked, turn. *(9 sts)*
Row 28: Ch 1, sk first st, sc in next st, dc in next st, cross st across next 6 sts. Fasten off. *(8 sts)*

Row 22: For **second shoulder**, with front of row 21 facing, join with sl st in opposite end of row, 21, rep row 22 of first shoulder, working cross sts as follows: sk next st, dc in next st, working in front of last dc, dc in sk st. *(21 sts)*

Rows 23–28: Rep rows 23–28: of first shoulder.

Bodice Back
Make 2.
Note: *Front of row 1 is RS of work on one back. Back of row 1 is RS of work on other back.*

Row 1: Ch 38, sc in second ch from hook and in each ch across, turn. *(37 sc)*

Row 2: Ch 3, cross st across, turn.

Rows 4 & 5: Rep rows 2 and 3.

Row 6: For **armhole**, ch 1, sc in each of first 4 sts dc in next st, cross st across with dc in last st, turn.

Row 7: Ch 1, sc in each st across leaving last 7 sts unworked, turn. *(30 sc)*

Row 8: Ch 3, cross st across with dc in last st, turn.

Row 9: Ch 1, sc in each st across leaving last st unworked, turn. *(29 sc)*

Row 10: Ch 3, cross st across, turn.

Row 11: Ch 1, sc in each st across, turn.

Rows 12–20: Rep rows 10 and 11 alternately, ending with row 10.

Row 21: Ch 1, sc in each st across with 2 sc in last st, turn. *(30 sc)*

Row 22: Ch 3, cross st across with dc in last st, turn.

Row 23: Ch 1, sc in each st across, turn.

Row 24: Rep row 22.

Row 25: Ch 1, sc in each st across, turn.

Row 26: For **shoulder shaping**, ch 1, sc in each of first 6 sts, dc in next st, cross st across with dc in last st, turn.

Row 27: Ch 1, sc in each st across, turn.

Row 28: Ch 3, cross st across next 14 sts leaving rem sts unworked for **neck edge**, turn. *(15 sts)*

Row 29: Ch 3, dc in each of next 3 sts, sc in each st across, turn.

Row 30: Ch 3, cross st across next 10 sts, [sk next st, tr in next st, tr in sk st] across. Fasten off.

Sew one back to each side of Front across ends of rows 1–6.

For shoulder seams, on each side, sew row 30 on back to tops of rows 26–28 on Front.

Skirt
Row 1: Working on opposite side of starting ch on Backs and Front, with RS facing, join with sl st in first ch at center back, ch 3, 2 dc in next ch, sk 1 ch at one seam and 2 chs at other seam, [dc in next ch, 2 dc in next ch] across, turn. *(210 dc)*

Note: *Reps may not work evenly across.*

Row 2: (Ch 3, dc) in first st, *ch 2, sk next 2 sts dc in each of next 2 sts, ch 2, sk next 2 sts, **V-st** *(see Special Stitches)* in next st, ch 2, sk next 2 sts, dc in next 2 sts, ch 2, sk next 2 sts, 2 dc in next st, ch 3, 2 dc in next st *(first shell made)*, rep from * around, ending last rep with 2 dc in last st, turn. *(60 dc, 14 V-sts, 13 shells)*

Rows 3 & 4: (Sl st, ch 3, dc) in sp between first 2 sts, sk each ch-2 sp, [ch 2, dc in each of next 2 sts, ch 2, V-st, ch 2, dc in each of next 2 sts, ch 2, **shell** *(see Special Stitches)*] around, ending last rep with 2 dc in sp between last 2 sts, turn.

Row 5: (Sl st, ch 3, dc) in sp between first 2 sts, sk each ch-2 sp, [ch 2, dc in next st, 2 dc in next st, ch 2, V-st, ch 2, 2 dc in next st, dc in next st, ch 2, shell] around, ending last rep with 2 dc in sp between last 2 sts, turn. *(88 dc, 14 V-sts, 13 shells)*

Row 6: (Sl st, ch 3, dc) in space between first 2 sts, sk each ch-2 sp, *ch 2, dc in each of next 3 sts, ch 2, (dc, ch 5, dc) in next ch-3 sp, ch 2, dc in each of next 3 sts, ch 2, shell, rep from * around, ending last rep with 2 dc in sp between last 2 sts, turn. *(116 dc, 14 ch-5 sps, 13 shells)*

Row 7: (Sl st, ch 3, dc) in sp between first 2 sts, sk each ch-2 sp, [ch 3, dc in each of next 3 sts, ch 1, 9 dc in next ch-5 sp, ch 1, dc in each of next 3 sts, ch 3, shell] around, ending last rep with 2 dc in sp between last 2 sts, turn. *(214 dc, 13 shells)*

Row 8: (Sl st, ch 3, dc) in sp between first 2 sts, sk each ch-2 sp, *ch 3, dc in each of next 3 sts, [ch 1, dc in next dc of dc-group] 9 times, ch 1, dc in each of next 3 sts, ch 3, shell, rep from * around, ending last rep with 2 dc in sp between last 2 sts, turn. *(214 dc, 140 ch-1 sps, 13 shells)*

Row 9: (Sl st, ch 3, dc) in sp between first 2 sts, *ch 3, 2 dc in next st, dc in each of next 2 sts, ch 3, sk next ch-1 sp, [dc in next ch-1 sp, ch 3] 8 times, dc in each of next 2 sts, 2 dc in next st, ch 3, shell, rep from * around, ending last rep with 2 dc in sp between last 2 sts, turn. *(116 dc, 154 ch-3 sps, 13 shells)*

Rnd 10: (Sl st, ch 3, dc) in sp between first 2 sts, *ch 3, dc in each of next 4 sts, ch 3, sk next ch-3 sp, [sl st in next ch-3 sp, ch 3] 7 times, dc in each of next 4 sts, ch 3, shell, rep from * around, ending last rep with 2 dc in sp between last 2 sts, ch 1, join with dc in top of first ch 3 *(ch 1, and dc count as joining ch sp)*, **turn**. *(116 dc, 140 ch-3 sps, 13 shells)*

Rnd 11: (Ch 3, dc, ch 3, 2 dc) in joining ch sp *(counts as first shell)*, *ch 3, dc in each of next 4 sts, ch 3, sk next ch-3 sp, [sl st in next ch-3 sp, ch 3] 6 times, dc in each of next 4 sts, ch 3, (shell, ch 3, shell) in next shell, rep from * around, ending last rep with shell in joining ch sp, ch 1, join with dc in top of beg ch-3. *(112 dc, 126 ch-3 sps, 28 shells)*

Rnd 12: Ch 3, dc in joining ch sp, shell in next ch-3 sp, *ch 3, dc in each of next 4 dc, ch 3, sk next ch sp, [sl st in next ch-3 sp, ch 3] 5 times, dc in each of next 4 dc, ch 3, sk next ch sp, shell in each of next 3 ch-3 sps, rep from * around, ending last rep with 2 dc in joining ch sp, ch 1, join with dc in top of beg ch-3. *(Joining ch sp with 2 dc on each side counts as shell.)* *(112 dc, 112 ch-3 sps, 42 shells)*

Rnd 13: Ch 3, dc in joining ch sp, shell, ch 3, sk next dc, 2 dc in last dc of shell, *ch 3, sk next dc, dc in each of next 3 dc, dc in next ch sp, ch 3, [sl st in next ch-3 sp, ch 3] 4 times, dc in next ch sp, dc in each of next 3 dc, sk next dc and next ch-3 sp, ch 3, 2 dc in next dc, ch 3, shell in each of next 3 ch-3 sps, ch 3, sk next dc, 2 dc in last dc of shell, rep from * around, ending last rep with 2 dc in joining ch sp, ch 1, join with dc in top of beg ch-3. *(168 dc, 126 ch-3 sps, 42 shells)*

Rnd 14: Ch 3, dc in joining ch sp, shell in each of next 2 ch sps, *ch 3, sk next dc, dc in each of next 3 dc, dc in next ch sp, ch 3, [sl st in next ch-3 sp, ch 3] 3 times, dc in next ch sp, dc in each of next 3 dc, sk next dc and next ch sp, ch 3, shell in each of next 5 ch-3 sps, rep from * around, ending last rep with 2 dc in joining ch sp, ch 1, join with dc in top of beg ch-3. *(112 dc, 84 ch-3 sps, 70 shells)*

Rnd 15: Ch 3, dc in joining ch sp, shell in each of next 2 ch sps, *ch 3, sc in next ch sp, ch 3, sk next dc, dc in each of next 3 dc, dc in next ch sp, ch 3, [sl st in next ch-3 sp, ch 3] twice, dc in next ch sp, dc in each of next 3 dc, sk next dc, ch 3, sc in next ch sp, ch 3, shell in each of next 5 ch-3 sps, rep from * around, ending last rep with 2 dc in joining ch sp, ch 1, join with dc in top of beg ch 3. *(112 dc, 98 ch-3 sps, 70 shells)*

Rnd 16: Ch 3, 2 dc in joining ch sp **L-shell** *(see Special Stitches)* in each of next 2 ch sps, [ch 1, 2 dc in next ch sp] twice, *ch 3, sk next dc, dc in each of next 3 dc, dc in next ch sp, ch 3, sl st in next ch-3 sp, ch 3, dc in next ch sp, dc in each of next 3 dc, sk next dc, ch 3, [2 dc in next ch sp, ch 1] twice, L-shell in each of next 5 ch-3 sps, rep from * around, ending last rep with 3 dc in joining ch sp, ch 1, join with dc in top of beg ch-3. *(224 dc, 56 ch-3 sps, 56 ch-1 sps, 70 L-shells)*

Rnd 17: Ch 3, 2 dc in joining ch sp, L-shell in each of next 2 ch sps, *2 dc in next ch sp, ch 3, 2 dc in each of next 2 ch sps, ch 3, sk next dc, dc in each of next 3 dc, dc in next ch sp, ch 3, dc in next ch sp, dc in each of next 3 dc, ch 3, sk next dc, 2 dc in each of next 2 ch sps, ch 3, 2 dc in next ch sp, L-shell in each of next 5 shells, rep from * around, ending last rep with 3 dc in joining ch sp, ch 1, join with dc in top of beg ch-3. *(70 ch sp, 70 L-shells)*

Rnd 18: Ch 3, 2 dc in joining ch sp, L-shell in each ch-3 sp around, ending with 3 dc in joining ch sp, ch 1, join with dc in top of beg ch 3. *(140 L-shells)*

Rnd 19: Ch 3, 2 dc in joining ch sp, L-shell in next ch-3 sp, (L-shell, ch 3, 3 dc) in next ch-3 sp, *L-shell in each of next 5 ch-3 sps, (L-shell, ch 3, 3 dc) in next ch-3 sp, L-shell in next ch-3 sp, (L-shell, ch 3, 3 dc) in next ch-3 sp, rep from * around, ending last rep with shell in joining ch sp, ch 1, join with dc in top of first ch-3. *(140 L-shells, 42 ch-3 sps)*

Rnds 20 & 21: Ch 3, 2 dc in joining ch sp, L-shell in each ch-3 sp around, ending with 3 dc in joining ch sp, ch 1, join with dc in top of beg ch-3. *(182 L-shells)*

Rnd 22: Ch 3, 2 dc in joining ch sp, L-shell in next ch-3 sp, (L-shell, ch 3, 3 dc) in next ch-3 sp, *L-shell in each of next 7 ch-3 sps, (L-shell, ch 3, 3 dc) in next ch-3 sp, L-shell, in next ch-3 sp, (L-shell, ch 3, 3 dc) in each of next 2 ch-3 sps, L-shell in next ch-3 sp, (L-shell, ch 3, 3 dc) in next ch-3 sp, rep from * around, ending last rep with L-shell in joining ch sp, ch 1, join with dc in top of beg ch-3.

Rnd 23: Ch 1, sc in first ch sp, ch 6, [sc in next sp between shells or in next ch-3 sp, ch 6] around, join with sl st in first sc. Fasten off.

Sleeve
Make 2.
Row 1: Ch 58, sc in second ch from hook and in each ch across, turn. *(57 sc)*

Row 2: Ch 4 *(counts as dc and ch 1)*, sk next st, dc in next st, [ch 1, sk next st, dc in next st] across, turn.

Rows 3 & 4: Ch 3, **V-st** *(see Special Stitches)* in each ch sp across with dc in last st, turn. *(2 dc, 28 V-sts)*

Row 5: Ch 3, dc in same st, **shell** *(see Special Stitches)* in next ch sp, [V-st in next ch sp, shell in next ch sp] across, ending with (V-st, 2 dc) in last st, turn. *(4 dc, 29 shells and V-sts)*

Row 6: For **cap of sleeve,** sl st in each of first 6 sts and chs, ch 2 *(sl sts and ch 2 are not worked into or counted as sts)*, V-st in each V-st and shell in each shell across to last ch sp, dc in last ch sp leaving rem sts unworked, turn. *(2 dc, 26 shells and V-sts)*

Row 7: Sl st in each of first 3 sts and chs, ch 2, dc in next dc, shell in each shell and V-st in each V-st across to last ch sp, dc in last ch sp, turn. *(2 dc, 24 shells and V-sts)*

Row 8: Ch 2, shell in each shell and V-st in each V-st across with dc in top of ch-2, turn. *(24 shells and V-sts)*

Row 9: Ch 2, dc in first ch sp, shell in each shell and V-st in each V-st across to last ch sp, dc in last ch sp, turn. *(2 dc, 22 shells and V-sts)*

Row 10: Sl st in each of first 9 sts and chs, ch 2, shell in each shell and V-st in each V-st across to last 2 ch sps, dc in next ch sp leaving rem sts unworked, turn. *(1 dc, 18 shells and V-sts)*

Rows 11–15: Rep rows 8 and 6 alternately, ending with row 8 and *(14 shells and V-sts)*.

Row 16: Sl st in sts and chs across to third ch sp, ch 2, dc in fourth ch sp, [shell in next shell, V-st in next V-st] 3 times, **dc dec** *(see Stitch Guide)* in next 2 ch sps leaving rem sts unworked, turn. *(1 dc, 6 shells and V-sts)*

Row 17: Sl st in each of first 4 sts and chs, ch 2, [shell in next shell,

V-st in next V-st] twice, dc dec in next ch sp and last st. Fasten off. *(1 dc, 4 shells and V-sts)*

Rnd 18: Join with sc in end of row 6, sc in ends of rows and in ch sps across cap of sleeve to other end of row 6 *(about 55 to 60 sts)*. Fasten off.

Sew ends of rows 1–5 tog at underarm.

Matching under seam to top of side seam on Bodice, gather cap of sleeve to fit, sew sleeve in armhole.

Finishing

1. For **Sleeve trim**, working around one Sleeve in opposite side of ch on row 1, join with sl st in seam, ch 4, [sl st in next ch, ch 4] around, join with sl st in first sl st. Fasten off. Rep on other Sleeve.

2. For **neck trim**, working sts and in ends of rows around neck edge, join with sl st at corner on back neck edge, ch 4, placing one sl st in each st and in end of each sc row and 2 sl sts in end of each dc or tr row, [sl st, ch 4] across neck edge to corner of back on other side. Fasten off.

3. Sew one ribbon rose to center of row 14 and one to center of row 18 on Bodice Front.

4. Lapping left Back over right Back, sew four snaps evenly spaced on center back edges between Bodice Backs, sew one button over each snap on outside of left Back.

5. Cut two 16-inch lengths of ribbon, weave one length through row 2 on each Sleeve, tie ends in bow at center of Sleeve.

BIB

Row 1: Ch 18, sc in second ch from hook and in each ch across, turn. *(17 sc)*

Rows 2–12: Ch 1, 2 sc in first st, sc in each st across with 2 sc in last st, turn, ending with *(39 sc)*.

Row 13: Ch 1, sc in each st across, turn.

Row 14: Ch 1, 2 sc in first sc, sc in each st across with 2 sc in last st, turn. *(41 sc)*

Rows 15–28: Ch 1, sc in each st across, turn.

Row 29: For **first strap**, ch 1, sc in each of first 16 sts leaving rem sts unworked, turn. *(16 sc)*

Row 30: Ch 1, sc in each st across, turn.

Row 31: Ch 1, sk first st, sc in each st across, turn. *(15 sc)*

Rows 32–41: Rep rows 30 and 31 alternately, ending with *(10 sc)*.

Rows 42–46: Ch 1, sc in each st across, turn.

Row 47: Ch 1, sc in each st across with 2 sc in last st, turn. *(11 sc)*

Row 48: Ch 1, 2 sc in first st, sc in each st across leaving last st unworked, turn.

Row 49: Ch 1, sc in each st across with 2 sc in last st, turn. *(12 sc)*

Row 50: Ch 1, sc in each st across, turn.

Row 51: Ch 1, sc in each st across with 2 sc in last st, turn. *(13 sc)*

Row 52: Ch 1, sc in each st across leaving last st unworked, turn. *(12 sc)*

Rows 53–55: Rep rows 51, 52, and 51, ending with *13 sc*.

Row 56: Ch 3, sc in second ch from hook, sc in next ch, sc in each st across leaving last st unworked, turn. *(14 sc)*

Row 57: Ch 1, sc in each st across, turn.

Rows 58–61: Rep rows 56 and 57 alternately, ending with *16 sc*.

Rows 62 & 63: Ch 1, sc in each st across leaving last st unworked, turn, ending with *14 sc*. Fasten off.

Row 29: For **second strap**, with RS of row 28 facing, join with sc in first st at opposite end of row 28, sc in each of next 15 sts leaving rem sts unworked, turn. *(16 sc)*

Rows 30–63: Rep rows 30–63 of first strap. At end of last row, **do not fasten off.**

For **lining**, using rows 1–44 as pattern, cut a piece of flexible vinyl ½ inch smaller than bib on all edges and lay aside.

Border

Rnd 1: Ch 1, working around outer edge, then neck edge, sc in each st and in end of each row around entire Bib, join with sl st in beg sc.

Rnd 2: Ch 1, sc in first st, (ch 4, sc) in each st around, ch 1, join with dc in beg sc.

Row 3: Working around outer edges only, (ch 4, sl st) in each ch sp around to last ch sp at end of other strap, **do not work neck edge**. Fasten off.

Trim

Row 1: Ch 12, sc in second ch from hook and in each ch across, turn. *(11 sc)*

Row 2: Ch 3, dc in same st, ch 2, 2 dc in next st, [sk next st, 2 dc in next st, ch 2, 2 dc in next st] across, turn.

Row 3: Sl st across to first ch sp, (ch 3, dc, ch 2, 2 dc) in ch sp, (ch 1, 2 dc, ch 2, 2 dc) in each ch sp across, turn.

Row 4: Sl st across to first ch sp, (ch 3, 2 dc, ch 2, 3 dc) in ch sp, sk each ch-1 sp, (ch 2, 3 dc, ch 2, 3 dc) in each ch-2 sp across, turn.

Row 5: Sl st across to first ch sp, (ch 3, 2 dc, ch 2, 3 dc) in ch sp, [ch 3, sk next ch sp, (3 dc, ch 2, 3 dc) in next ch sp] across, turn.

Row 6: Sl st across to first ch sp, (ch 3, 2 dc, ch 2, 3 dc) in ch sp, [ch 3, sk next ch sp, (3 tr, ch 2, 3 tr) in next ch sp] twice, ch 3, sk next ch sp, (3 dc, ch 2, 3 dc) in last ch sp, turn.

Row 7: Sl st across to first ch sp, (ch 3, 2 dc, ch 3, 3 dc) in ch sp, [ch 4, sk next ch sp, (3 tr, ch 3, 3 tr) in next ch sp] twice, ch 4, sk next ch sp, (3 dc, ch 3, 3 dc) in last ch sp. Fasten off.

Finishing

1. Fuse flexible vinyl lining centered on back of Bib according to manufacturer's instructions.

2. Matching row 1 of center of row 28 on Bib, tack Trim to Bib being careful not to puncture vinyl backing.

3. Tack three ribbon roses to Bib through openings on row 7 of Trim.

4. Sew snap between ends of straps.

5. Tie rem 10-inch length of ribbon into a 1½-inch bow. Tack to center of row 1 on Trim. ❑❑

Pineapple Lace Top

Design by Suzann Thompson

SKILL LEVEL
■■■□ EXPERIENCED

FINISHED SIZE
Lady's medium, bust size 36 to 38

FINISHED CHEST MEASUREMENT
42 inches

MATERIALS
- DMC Cebelia crochet cotton size 10 (282 yds/50g per ball): 10 balls ecru
- Size 00/2.70mm steel crochet hook or size needed to obtain gauge
- Tapestry needle

GAUGE
15 sts and 7 rows = 3⅛ inches wide and 2½ inches long
Check gauge to save time.

PATTERN STITCH
Multiple of 15 sts + 1, add 2 for beg ch

Base row: 2 dc in third ch from hook, *ch 7, sk next 5 chs, sc in next ch, ch 3, sk next 2 chs, sc in next ch, ch 7, sk next 5 chs**, (2 dc, ch 1, 2 dc) in next ch, rep from * for pattern, ending last rep at **, 3 dc in last ch, turn.

Row 1: Ch 3 (counts as first dc), 2 dc in same dc, *ch 3, sc in next ch-7 sp, ch 2, tr in next ch-3 sp, ch 2, sc in next ch-7 sp, ch 3**, (2 dc, ch 1, 2 dc) in next ch-1 sp*, rep between * for pattern, ending last rep at **, 3 dc in turning ch, turn.

Row 2: Ch 3, 2 dc in same dc, *5 tr in next ch-2 sp, tr in next st, 5 tr in next ch-2 sp**, (2 dc, ch 1, 2 dc) in next ch-1 sp*, rep between * for pattern, ending last rep at **, 3 dc in last st, turn.

Row 3: Ch 3, 2 dc in same dc, *ch 2, sk next 2 dc, sc in next tr, [ch 3, sk next tr, sc in next tr] 5 times, ch 2, sk next 2 dc**, (2 dc, ch 1, 2 dc) in next ch-1 sp, rep from * for pattern, ending last rep at **, 3 dc in last st, turn.

Row 4: Ch 3, 2 dc in same dc, *ch 3, sk next 2 chs, sc in next ch-3 sp, [ch 3, sc in next ch-3 sp] 4 times, ch 3, sk next 2 chs**, (2 dc, ch 1, 2 dc) in next ch-1 sp, rep between * for pattern, ending last rep at **, 3 dc in last st, turn.

Row 5: Ch 3, 2 dc in same dc, *ch 4, sk next 3 chs, sc in next ch-3 sp, [ch 3, sc in next ch-3 sp] 3 times, ch 4, sk next 3 chs**, (2 dc, ch 1, 2 dc) in next ch-1 sp, rep from * for pattern, ending last rep at **, 3 dc in last st, turn.

Row 6: Ch 3, 2 dc in same dc, *ch 5, sk next 4 chs, sc in next ch-3 sp, [ch 3, sc in next ch-3 sp] twice, ch 5, sk next 4 chs**, (2 dc, ch 1, 2 dc) in next ch-1 sp*, rep between * for pattern, ending last rep at **, 3 dc in last st, turn.

Row 7: Ch 3, 2 dc in same dc, *ch 7, sk next 5 chs, sc in next ch-3 sp, ch 3, sc in next ch-3 sp, ch 7, sk next 5 chs**, (2 dc, ch 1, 2 dc) in next ch-1 sp, rep from * for pattern, ending last rep at **, 3 dc in last st, turn.

Rep rows 1–7 for pattern.

INSTRUCTIONS
BACK
Loosely ch 108, beg at shoulders, work even in pattern until piece measures approximately 26 inches from beg, ending last pattern rep after Pattern Stitch row 3. Fasten off.

RIGHT FRONT
Ch 33, beg at right shoulder, work in Pattern Stitch, beg with base row, working rows 1–7 once.

RIGHT NECK INCREASE
Row 1: Work Pattern Stitch row 1 to **, ending with (2 dc, ch 1, 2 dc) in last st, turn.
Row 2: Ch 4, sk next 2 dc, (2 dc, ch 1, 2 dc) in first ch-1 sp, work Pattern Stitch row 2 from *.
Row 3: Work Pattern Stitch row 3 to **, ending with (2 dc, ch 1, 2 dc) in next ch-1 sp, ch 2, sk next 2 dc, sc in third ch of turning ch-4, turn.
Row 4: Ch 5, sc in third ch from hook, ch 3, sk next 2 dc, (2 dc, ch 1, 2 dc) in next ch-1 sp, work Pattern Stitch row 4 from *.
Row 5: Work Pattern Stitch row 5 across to **, ending with (2 dc, ch 1, 2 dc) in next ch-1 sp, ch 4, sk next 2 dc, sc in third ch of turning ch-5, turn.
Row 6: Ch 5, sc in third ch from hook, ch 5, sk next 2 dc, (2 dc, ch 1, 2 dc) in next ch-1 sp, work Pattern Stitch row 6 from *.
Row 7: Work Pattern Stitch row 7 to **, ending with (2 dc, ch 1, 2 dc) in next ch-1 sp, ch 7, sk next 2 dc, sc in third of turning ch-5, ch 2, turn. Fasten off.

LEFT FRONT
Ch 33, beg at left shoulder work in Pattern Stitch, beg with base row, work rows 1–7 once.

LEFT NECK INCREASE
Row 1: Ch 5, 2 dc in first st, work Pattern Stitch row 1, from *.
Row 2: Work Pattern Stitch row 2 to **, (2 dc, ch 1, 2 dc) in turning ch sp from previous row, turn.
Row 3: Ch 5, sk next 4 chs, sc in next ch of turning ch, ch 2, sk next 2 dc, (2 dc, ch 1, 2 dc) in next ch-1 sp, work Pattern Stitch row 3 from *.
Row 4: Work Pattern Stitch row 4, rep between * twice, ending with ch 3, sc in turning ch sp from previous row, turn.
Row 5: Ch 5, sk next 3 chs, sc in next ch of turning ch, ch 4, sk next 2 dc, (2 dc, ch 1, 2 dc) in next ch-1 sp, work Pattern Stitch row 5 from *.
Row 6: Work Pattern Stitch row 6, rep between * twice, ending with ch 5, sc in turning ch sp from previous row, turn.
Row 7: Ch 7, sk next 5 chs, sc in next ch of turning ch, ch 7, sk next 2 dc, (2 dc, ch 1, 2 dc) in next ch-1 sp, work Pattern Stitch row 7 from *.
Row 8: Work Pattern Stitch row 1, rep between * twice, ending with ch 3, sc in next ch-7 sp, ch 2, tr in turning ch sp from previous row, ch 25, pick up right shoulder as if to work next row, tr in first st, ch 2, sc in next ch-7 sp, ch 3, sk next 2 dc, (2 dc, ch 1, 2 dc) in next ch-1 sp, work Pattern Stitch row 1 from *.
Row 9: Work Pattern Stitch row 2, rep between * twice, 5 tr in next ch-2 sp, tr in next tr, 2 tr in next ch of ch-25, tr in next ch, 2 tr in next ch, sk next 2 chs, 2 dc in next ch, ch 1, 2 dc in next ch, sk next 2 chs, [2 tr in next ch, tr in next ch] 3 times, 2 tr in next ch, sk next 2 chs, 2 dc in next ch, ch 1, 2 dc in next ch, sk next 2 chs, 2 tr in next ch, tr in next ch, 2 tr in next ch, tr in next tr, 5 tr in next ch-2 sp, (2 dc, ch 1, 2 dc) in next ch-1 sp, rep from * to end of row 2 of Pattern Stitch.

Next rows: Continue in pattern as established, beg with Pattern Stitch row 3, until piece measure same length as Back, ending last pattern rep after Pattern Stitch row 3. At end of last row, fasten off.
Sew Front to Back at shoulders.

NECK FINISHING
Join with sl st at shoulder seam, ch 1, sc in same place, [ch 3, sc in next ch sp] around, ending with ch 3, join with sl st in beg sc. Fasten off.

SLEEVE
Make 2.
Ch 93, work Pattern Stitch Base row and rows 1–7.

Sleeve Decrease
Row 1: Work Pattern Stitch row 1.
Row 2: Ch 3, sk next 2 dc, next ch-2 sp and next sc, *5 tr in next ch-2 sp, tr in next st, 5 tr in next ch-2 sp**, (2 dc, ch 1, 2 dc) in next ch-1 sp, rep from * for pattern, ending last rep at **, ch 3, sl st in last st, turn.
Row 3: Sl st in each of next 3 chs, ch 1, *sc in next tr, [ch 3, sk next tr, sc in next tr] 5 times**, ch 2, sk next 2 dc, (2 dc, ch 1, 2 dc) in next ch-1 sp, ch 2, sk next 2 dc, sc in next tr, rep from * for pattern ending last rep at **, turn.
Row 4: Sl st in next sc, (sl st, ch 1, sc) in next ch-3 sp, *[ch 3, sc in next ch-3 sp] 4 times**, ch 3, (2 dc, ch 1, 2 dc) in next ch-1 sp, ch 3, sk next ch-2 sp, sc in next ch-3 sp, rep from * for pattern, ending last rep at **, turn.
Row 5: Sl st in next sc, (sl st, ch 1, sc) in next ch-3 sp, *[ch 3, sc in next ch-3 sp] 3 times**, ch 4, sk next 3 chs, (2 dc, ch 1, 2 dc) in next ch-1 sp, ch 4, sk next ch-3 sp, sc in next ch-3 sp, rep from * for pattern, ending last rep at **, turn.
Row 6: Sl st in next sc, (sl st, ch 1, sc) in next ch-3 sp, *[ch 3, sc in next ch-3 sp] twice**, ch 5, sk next ch-4 sp, (2 dc, ch 1, 2 dc) in next ch-1 sp, ch 5, sk next ch-4 sp, sc in next ch-3 sp, rep from

* for pattern, ending last rep at **, turn.

Row 7: Sl st in next sc, (sl st, ch 1, sc) in next ch-3 sp, *ch 3, sc in next ch-3 sp**, ch 7, sk next ch-5 sp, (2 dc, ch 1, 2 dc) in next ch-1 sp, ch 7, sk next ch-5 sp, sc in next ch-3 sp, rep from * for pattern, ending last rep at **, turn.

Row 8: Sl st in next sc, sl st in first ch-3 sp, ch 6, *sc in next ch-7 sp, ch 3, (2 dc, ch 1, 2 dc) in next ch-1 sp, ch 3, sc in next ch-7 sp, ch 2, tr in next ch-3 sp**, ch 2, rep from * for pattern, ending last rep at **, turn.

Sleeve continues even for several rows.

Row 9: Ch 4, *5 tr in next ch-2 sp, (2 dc, ch 1, 2 dc) in next ch-1 sp, sk next 2 dc, 5 tr in next ch-2 sp, tr in next tr, rep from * for pattern, turn.

Row 10: Ch 3, *[sc in next tr, ch 3, sk next tr] twice, sc in next tr, ch 2, sk next 2 dc**, (2 dc, ch 1, 2 dc) in next ch-1 sp, ch 2, sk next 2 dc, [sc in next tr, ch 3, sk next tr] twice, sc in next tr, rep from * for pattern, ending with ch 1, hdc in fourth st of turning ch-4 turn.

Row 11: Ch 1, sc in first st, *[ch 3, sc in next ch-3 sp] twice, ch 3, sk next 2 chs**, (2 dc, ch 1, 2 dc) in next ch-1 sp, sk next 2 chs**, [ch 3, sc in next ch-3 sp] twice, rep from * for pattern, ending with ch 2, sc in second ch of turning ch-3 turn.

Row 12: *[Ch 3, sc in next ch-3 sp] twice, ch 4, sk next ch-3 sp, (2 dc, ch 1, 2 dc) in next ch-1 sp, ch 4, sk next ch-3 sp, sc in next ch-3 sp, ch 3, sc in next ch-3 sp, rep from * for pattern, ending with ch 1, hdc in last st, turn.

Row 13: Ch 1, sc in first st, *ch 3, sc in next ch-3 sp, ch 5, sk next ch-4 sp**, (2 dc, ch 1, 2 dc) in next ch-1 sp, ch 5, sk next ch-4 sp, sc in next ch-3 sp, ch 3, sc in next ch-3 sp, rep from * for pattern, ending with ch 2, sc in second ch of turning, ch-3 turn.

Row 14: *Ch 3, sc in next ch-3 sp, ch 7, sk next ch-5 sp, (2 dc, ch 1, 2 dc) in next ch-1 sp, ch 7, sk next ch-5 sp, sc in next ch-3 sp, rep from * for pattern, ending with ch 1, hdc in last st, turn.

Row 15: Ch 6, *sc in next ch-7 sp, ch 3, (2 dc, ch 1, 2 dc) in next ch-1 sp, ch 3, sc in next ch-7 sp, ch 2, tr in next ch-3 sp, ch 2, rep from * for pattern, ending with tr in second ch of turning ch-3, turn.

Rows 16–20: Rep rows 9–13.

Row 21: Sl st in next sc, (sl st, ch 1, sc) in next ch-3 sp, *ch 7, sk next 5 chs, (2 dc, ch 1, 2 dc) in next ch-1 sp, ch 7, sk next 5 chs, sc in next ch-3 sp**, ch 3, sc in next ch-3 sp, rep from * for pattern, ending last rep at ** turn.

Row 22: Sl st in first st and in each of next 3 chs, ch 1, sc in next ch-7 sp, *ch 3, (2 dc, ch 1, 2 dc) in next ch-1 sp, ch 3, sc in next ch-7 sp**, ch 2, tr in next ch-3 sp, ch 2, sc in next ch-7 sp, rep from * for pattern, ending last rep at **, turn.

Row 23: Ch 4, sk next ch-3 sp and next 2 dc, *(2 dc, ch 1, 2 dc) in next ch-1 sp**, 5 tr in next ch-2 sp, tr in next tr, 5 tr in next ch-2 sp, rep from * for pattern, ending last rep at **, ch 4, sl st in beg sc of previous row, turn.

Row 24: Sl st in each of next 4 chs, sl st in each of next 2 dc, (sl st, ch 3, 2 dc) in next ch-1 sp, *ch 2, sk next 2 dc, sc in next tr, [ch 3, sk next tr, sc in next tr] 5 times, ch 2, sk next 2 dc**, (2 dc, ch 1, 2 dc) in next ch-1 sp, rep from * for pattern, ending last rep at **, 3 dc in next ch-1 sp, turn.

Rows 25–28: Rep Pattern Stitch rows 4–7.

Rows 29–38: Rep Sleeve Decrease rows 1–10. At end of last row, fasten off.

FINISHING

Measure 9 inches down from shoulders on each edge of Front and Back pieces, mark 9-inch point with marker.

Sew Sleeve to one side of body, with top corner of Sleeve at one marker, center top of Sleeve at shoulder seam and other top corner of Sleeve at other marker.

Sew Sleeve and underarm seam.

Rep for other Sleeve. Rep neck finishing around bottom of Top and Sleeves.

Potpourri Bowl

Design by Mrs. H. Kaufman

SKILL LEVEL
 INTERMEDIATE

FINISHED SIZE
10 inches across

MATERIALS
- Crochet cotton size 10: 242 yds white
- Size 8/1.50mm steel crochet hook or size needed to obtain gauge
- ¾ yd ¼-inch-wide satin ribbon
- Lint-free fabric: enough to cover bowl
- 5½-inch deep x 10-inch diameter bowl
- Fabric stiffener
- Rustproof straight pins

GAUGE
9 chs = 1 inch, 9 sts = 1 inch, 5 dc rows = 2 inches

SPECIAL STITCHES
2-dc shell: (2 dc, ch 1, 2 dc) in next st or ch sp.
Beginning 2-dc shell (beg 2-dc shell), (Ch 3–*counts as first dc*, dc, ch 1, 2 dc) in same st or sp.
3-dc shell: (3 dc, ch 2, 3 dc) in next st or ch sp.
Beginning 3-dc shell (beg 3-dc shell): (Ch 3, 2 dc, ch 2, 3 dc) in same ch sp or st.
Beginning shell increase (beg shell inc): (Ch 3, 2 dc, {ch 1, 3 dc} twice) in same ch sp.
Shell increase (shell inc): (3 dc, {ch 1, 3 dc} twice) in next shell.

INSTRUCTIONS
DOILY
Rnd 1: Ch 8, sl st in beg ch to form ring, ch 4 *(counts as first tr)*, 31 tr in ring, join with sl st in fourth ch of beg ch-4. *(32 tr)*
Row 2: Now working in rows, for **first block,** ch 11, sc in second ch from hook, sc in each of next 8 chs, leaving rem ch unworked, turn. *(9 sc)*

Row 3: Ch 2 *(counts as first hdc)*, hdc in each st across, turn. *(9 hdc)*
Row 4: Ch 2, hdc in each st across, ch 10, sk next 3 sts on rnd 1, sc in next st, turn. *(10 sc, 10 chs)*
Row 5: For **next block,** ch 1, sc in each of first 9 chs, leaving rem ch unworked, turn. *(9 sc, 1 ch)*
Rows 6 & 7: Ch 1, sc in each st across, turn.
Rows 8–31: Rep rows 4–7 consecutively.
Row 32: Ch 1, sc in each st across, ch 1, sl st in bottom of first st on row 2 at bottom corner of first block.
Rnd 33: Now working in rnds, ch 3 *(counts as first dc)*, sc in first st on row 4 at top corner of first block, ch 7, [tr in ch between blocks, ch 3, sc in first st on last row at top corner of next block, ch 7] 7 times, tr in ch between blocks, ch 3, join with sl st in third ch of beg ch-3, **turn.** *(8 tr, 8 sc, 80 chs)*
Rnd 34: Ch 3, dc in each ch and in each st around, join. *(96 dc)*
Rnd 35: Beg 2-dc shell *(see Special Stitches)*, ch 7, sk next 5 sts, [**2-dc shell** *(see Special Stitches)* in next st, ch 7, sk next 5 sts] around, join, sl st in next st, sl st in next ch sp, turn. *(16 shells, 16 ch sps)*
Rnd 36: Beg 2-dc shell, ch 7, [2-dc shell in ch sp of next shell, ch 7] around, join, sl st in next st, sl st in next ch sp, turn.
Rnd 37: Beg 2-dc shell, ch 3, sc around ch-7 chs of last 2 rnds at the same time, [2-dc shell in next shell, ch 3, sc around ch-7 chs of last 2 rnds at the same time, ch 3] around, join, sl st in next st, sl st in next ch sp, turn. *(16 shells, 16 sc, 32 ch sps)*
Rnd 38: (Ch 3, 2 dc, ch 1, 3 dc) in same ch sp, ch 5, 11 dc in next shell, ch 5, [(3 dc, ch 1, 3 dc) in next shell, ch 5, 11 dc in next shell, ch 5] around, join, sl st in each of next 2 sts, sl st in next ch sp, turn.
Rnd 39: (Ch 3, 2 dc, ch 1, 3 dc) in same ch sp, *ch 5, dc in sp between next 2 dc, [ch 1, dc in next sp between dc] 9 times, ch 5**, (3 dc, ch 1, 3 dc) in next ch-1 sp, rep from * around, ending last rep at **, join, sl st in each of next 2 sts, sl st in next ch sp, turn.
Rnd 40: Beg 3-dc shell *(see Special Stitches)* in same sp, *ch 5, dc in next ch-1 sp, [ch 1, dc in next ch-1 sp] 8 times, ch 5**, **3-dc shell** *(see Special Stitches)* in next ch-1 sp, rep from * around, ending last rep at **, join, sl st in each of next 2 chs, sl st in next ch sp, turn.

Rnd 41: Beg 3-dc cl in same ch sp, *ch 6, dc in next ch-1 sp, [ch 1, dc in next ch-1 sp] 7 times, ch 6**, shell in next shell, rep from * around, ending last rep at **, join, sl st in each of next 2 sts, sl st in next ch sp, turn.

Rnd 42: Beg shell inc *(see Special Stitches),* *ch 7, dc in next ch-1 sp, [ch 1, dc in next ch-1 sp] 6 times, ch 7**, **shell inc,** *(see Special Stitches),* rep from * around, ending last rep at **, sl st in each of next 2 sts, sl st in next ch sp, turn.

Row 43: Now working in rows, for **first point,** beg 3-dc shell, ch 7, dc in next ch-1 sp, [ch 1, dc in next ch-1 sp] 5 times, ch 7, 3-dc shell in next ch-1 sp, ch 5, sl st in next dc, leaving rem sts unworked, turn.

Row 44: Ch 1, 7 dc in first ch-5 sp, sl st in each of next 3 sts, sl st in next ch sp, beg 3-dc shell, ch 6, sc in next ch-1 sp, [ch 1, dc in next ch sp] 4 times, ch 6, 3-dc shell in last shell, ch 5, sl st in last dc on previous row, turn.

Rows 45–47: Ch 1, 7 sc in first ch-5 sp, sl st in each of next 3 sts, sl st in next ch sp, beg 3-dc shell, ch 6, sk next ch-6 sp, dc in next ch-1 sp, [ch 1, dc in next ch-1 sp] across to next ch-6 sp, ch 6, sk next ch-6 sp, shell in last shell, ch 5, sl st in last dc on previous row, turn.

Row 48: Ch 1, 7 dc in first ch-5 sp, sl st in each of next 3 sts, sl st in next ch sp, beg 3-dc shell, ch 6, sk next ch-6 sp, dc in next ch-1 sp, ch 6, sk next ch-6 sp, 3-dc shell in last shell, ch 5, sl st in last dc of previous row, turn.

Row 49: Ch 1, 7 sc in first ch-5 sp, sl st in each of next 3 sts, sl st in next ch sp, **turn,** ch 8, sl st in last dc of shell on previous row, **turn,** 7 sc in ch-8 sp, (2 dc, ch 2, 3 dc) in same sp of first shell, sk next 2 ch-6 sps, 3-dc shell in last shell, ch 5, sl st in last dc of previous row, turn.

Row 50: Ch 1, 7 sc in first ch-5 sp, sl st in each of next 3 sts, sl st in next ch sp, ch 7, sl st in last shell, turn.

Row 51: Ch 1, 10 sc in first ch-7 sp, leaving rem sts unworked. Fasten off.

For **second through eighth points,** join with sl st in next ch sp of shell increase, on rnd 42; work same as first point.

FINISHING

1. Place fabric tightly over bottom of 10-inch bowl, tape to inside of bowl to secure.
2. Apply fabric stiffener to crocheted bowl according to manufacturer's instructions. Place over fabric-covered bowl and shape. Pin in place. Let dry completely.
3. Decorate with ribbon as desired.❑❑

Regency Centerpiece

Design by Judy Teague Treece

SKILL LEVEL
■■■☐ INTERMEDIATE

FINISHED SIZE
19½ inches in diameter

MATERIALS
❑ Crochet cotton size 10 (450 yds per ball):
   1 ball natural
❑ Size 6/1.80mm steel crochet hook or size needed to obtain gauge

GAUGE
Rnds 1–3 = 1¾ inches in diameter

SPECIAL STITCHES
V-stitch (V-st): (Dc, ch 2, dc) in indicated sp or st.
Shell: (2 dc, ch 2, 2 dc) in indicated sp or st.
3-double crochet cluster (3-dc cl): Yo, insert hook in st or ch sp, yo, pull lp through, yo, pull through 2 lps on hook, [yo, insert hook in same st or ch sp, yo, pull lp through, yo, pull through 2 lps on hook] twice, yo, pull through all lps on hook.

Beginning 3-double crochet cluster (beg 3-dc cl): Ch 2; Yo, insert hook in st or ch sp, yo, pull lp through, yo, pull through

2 lps on hook, yo, insert hook in same st or ch sp, yo, pull lp through, yo, pull through 2 lps on hook, yo, pull through all lps on hook.

Cluster shell (cl shell): (dc cl, ch 3, dc cl) in indicated sp or st.

Beginning cluster shell (beg cl shell): (Beg dc cl, ch 3, dc cl) in indicated sp or st.

Double cluster shell (double cl shell): (dc cl, ch 3, cl shell) in indicated sp or st.

Beginning double cluster shell (beg double cl shell): (Beg dc cl, ch 3, cl shell) in indicated sp or st.

INSTRUCTIONS
DOILY

Rnd 1: Ch 8, sl st in first ch to form ring, ch 3 *(counts as first dc throughout)*, 23 dc in ring, join with sl st in third ch of beg ch-3. *(24 dc)*

Rnd 2: Ch 1, sc in first st, ch 2, [sc in next dc, ch 2] around, join with sl st in beg sc. *(24 ch-2 sps)*

Rnd 3: Sl st into first ch sp, ch 3, dc in same ch sp, ch 2, [sk next ch sp, 2 dc in next ch sp, ch 2] around, join with sl st in third ch of beg ch-3. *(24 dc)*

Rnd 4: Ch 3, 2 dc in next dc, ch 2, [dc in next dc, 2 dc in next dc, ch 2] around, join.

Rnd 5: Ch 3, 2 dc in next dc, dc in next dc, ch 3, [dc in next dc, 2 dc in next dc, dc in next dc, ch 3] around, join.

Rnd 6: Ch 3, dc in next dc, 2 dc in next dc, dc in next dc, ch 3, [dc in each of next 2 dc, 2 dc in next dc, dc in next dc, ch 3] around, join.

Rnd 7: Ch 3, dc in each of next 2 dc, 2 dc in next dc, dc in next dc, ch 4, [dc in each of next 3 dc, 2 dc in next dc, dc in next dc, ch 4] around, join.

Rnd 8: Ch 3, dc in each of next 5 dc, *ch 3, sc in next sp, ch 3**, dc in each of next 6 dc, rep from * around, ending last rep at **, join.

Rnd 9: Ch 3, dc in next dc, *** dc dec** *(see Stitch Guide)* in next 2 sts, dc in each of next 2 dc, ch 3, sc in next ch sp, ch 2, sc in next ch sp, ch 3**, dc in each of next 2 dc, rep from * around, ending last rep at **, join.

Rnd 10: Ch 3, dc in next dc, *ch 2, sk next st, dc in each of next 2 dc, ch 3, **V-st** *(see Special Stitches)* in next ch-2 sp, ch 3**, dc in each of next 2 dc, rep from * around, ending last rep at **, join.

Rnd 11: Ch 3, dc in next dc, *ch 2, dc in each of next 2 dc, ch 3, **shell** *(see Special Stitches)* in next V-st, ch 3, sk next ch sp**, dc in each of next 2 dc, rep from * around, ending last rep at **, join.

Rnd 12: Ch 3, dc in next dc, *ch 2, dc in each of next 2 dc, ch 3, (sc, ch 6, sc) in next shell, ch 3, sk next ch sp**, dc in each of next 2 dc, rep from * around, ending last rep at **, join.

Rnd 13: Ch 3, dc in next dc, *ch 2, sc in next ch sp, ch 2, dc in each of next 2 dc, ch 1, 9 dc in next ch-6 sp, ch 1**, dc in each of next 2 dc, rep from * around, ending last rep at **, join.

Rnd 14: Sl st in next dc and in next ch sp, ch 1, sc in same ch sp, *ch 3, sc in next ch sp, ch 3, sc in first dc of next 9-dc group, [ch 2, sc in next dc] 8 times, ch 3**, sc in next ch-2 sp, rep from * around, ending last rep at **, join with sl st in beg sc.

Rnd 15: Sl st in next ch sp, **beg dc cl** *(see Special Stitches)* in same sp, *ch 2, sk next ch sp, [sc in next ch-2 sp, ch 2] 8 times, sk next ch-3 sp**, dc cl in next ch sp, rep from * around, ending last rep at **, join with sl st in top of beg dc cl.

Rnd 16: Ch 1, sc in first st, *ch 3, sk next ch-2 sp, sc in next ch-2 sp, [ch 2, sc in next ch-2 sp] 6 times, ch 3**, sc in top of next dc cl, rep from * around, ending last rep at **, join with sl st in beg sc.

Rnd 17: Sl st in next ch-3 sp, ch 1, sc in same ch sp, *ch 3, sc in next ch-2 sp, [ch 2, sc in next ch-2 sp] 5 times, ch 3, sc in next ch-3 sp**, ch 3, sc in next ch-3 sp, rep from * around, ending last rep at **, ch 1, hdc in beg sc to form last ch-3 sp.

Rnd 18: **Beg cl shell** *(see Special Stitches)* in ch sp just formed, *ch 3, sc in next ch-2 sp, [ch 2, sc in next ch-2 sp] 4 times, ch 3, sk next ch-3 sp**, **cl shell** *(see Special Stitches)* in next ch-3 sp, rep from * around, ending last rep at **, join with sl st in top of beg dc cl.

Rnd 19: Sl st in beg cl shell sp, **beg dbl cl shell** *(see Special Stitches)* in same ch sp, *ch 3, sc in next ch-2 sp, [ch 2, sc in next ch-2 sp] 3 times, ch 3**, **dbl cl shell** *(see Special Stitches)* in next shell, rep from * around, ending last rep at **, join with sl st in top of beg dc cl.

Rnd 20: Sl st in next ch-3 sp, beg cl shell in same ch sp, *ch 2, cl shell in next ch-3 sp, ch 3, sc in next ch-2 sp, [ch 2, sc in next ch-2 sp] twice, ch 3, sk next ch-3 sp**, cl shell in next ch-3 sp, rep from * around, ending last rep at **, join.

Rnd 21: Sl st in beg cl shell sp, beg cl shell in same ch sp, *ch 4, cl shell in next cl shell, ch 3, sk next ch-3 sp, sc in next ch-2 sp, ch 2, sc in next ch-2 sp, ch 3**, cl shell in next cl shell, rep from * around, ending last rep at **, join.

Rnd 22: Sl st in cl shell sp, beg cl shell in same ch sp, *ch 2, 7 dc in next ch-4 sp, ch 2, cl shell in next cl shell, ch 4, sc in next ch-2 sp, ch 4**, cl shell in next cl shell, rep from * around, ending last rep at **, join.

Rnd 23: Sl st in beg cl shell, beg cl shell in same ch sp, *ch 2, [sc in next dc, ch 2] 7 times, ch shell in next cl shell, ch 2**, cl shell in next cl shell, rep from * around, ending last rep at **, join.

Rnd 24: Sl st in beg cl shell, beg cl shell in same ch sp, *ch 2, sk next ch-2 sp, [sc in next ch-2 sp, ch 2] 6 times, cl shell in next cl shell, ch 2**, cl shell in next cl shell, rep from * around, ending last rep at **, join.

Rnd 25: Sl st in beg cl shell, beg cl shell in same ch sp, *ch 3, sk next ch-2 sp, sc in next ch-2 sp, [ch 2, sc in next ch-2 sp] 4 times, ch 3, cl shell in next cl shell, ch 2, sc in next sp, ch 2**, cl shell in next cl shell, rep from * around, ending last rep at **, join.

Rnd 26: Sl st in beg cl shell, beg cl shell in same ch sp, *ch 4, sc in next ch-2 sp, [ch 2, sc in next ch-2 sp] 3 times, ch 4, cl shell in next cl shell, ch 4**, cl shell in next cl shell, rep from * around, ending last rep at **, join.

Rnd 27: Sl st in beg cl shell, beg cl shell in same ch sp, *ch 5, sc in next ch-2 sp, [ch 2, sc in next ch-2 sp] twice, ch 5, cl shell in next cl shell, ch 3, sc in next ch sp, ch 3**, cl shell in next cl shell, rep from * around, ending last rep at **, join.

Rnd 28: Sl st in beg cl shell, beg cl shell in same ch sp, *ch 6, sc in next ch-2 sp, ch 2, sc in next ch-2 sp, ch 6, cl shell in next cl shell, [ch 3, sc in next ch sp] twice, ch 3**, cl shell in next cl shell, rep from * around, ending last rep at **, join.

Rnd 29: Sl st in beg cl shell, beg cl shell in same ch sp, *ch 7, sc in next ch-2 sp, ch 7, cl shell in next cl shell, [ch 4, sc in next ch sp] 3 times, ch 4**, cl shell in next cl shell, rep from * around, ending last rep at **, join.

Rnd 30: Sl st in beg cl shell, beg cl shell in same ch sp, *ch 5, cl shell in next cl shell, ch 2, cl shell in next sp, ch 2, sc in next ch sp, ch 6, sc in next ch sp, ch 2, cl shell in next ch sp, ch 2**, cl shell in next cl shell, rep from * around, ending last rep at **, join.

Rnd 31: Sl st in beg cl shell, beg cl shell in same ch sp, *ch 3, sc in ch-5 sp, ch 3, ch shell in next cl shell, ch 3, sc in next cl shell, ch 3, 7 dc in ch-6 sp, ch 3, sc in next cl shell, ch 3**, cl shell in next cl shell, rep from * around, ending last rep at **, join.

Rnd 32: Sl st in beg cl shell, beg cl shell in same ch sp, *ch 3, [sc in next sp, ch 3] twice, cl shell in next cl shell, ch 3, sc in next ch sp, ch 4, sc in next dc, [ch 2, sc in next dc] 6 times, ch 4, sk next ch sp, sc in next ch sp, ch 3**, cl shell in next cl shell, rep from * around, ending last rep at **, join.

Rnd 33: Sl st in beg cl shell, beg cl shell in same ch sp, *ch 2, sk next ch sp, V-st in next ch sp, ch 2, cl shell in next cl shell, ch 3, sc in next ch sp, ch 4, sk next ch sp, sc in next ch-2 sp, [ch 2, sc in next ch-2 sp] 5 times, ch 4, sk next ch sp, sc in next ch sp, ch 3**, cl shell in next cl shell, rep from * around, ending last rep at **, join.

Rnd 34: Sl st in beg cl shell, beg cl shell in same ch sp, *ch 2, shell in next V-st, ch 3, cl shell in next cl shell, ch 3, sc in next ch sp, ch 4, sk next ch sp, sc in next ch-2 sp, [ch 2, sc in next ch-2 sp] 4 times, ch 4, sk next ch sp, sc in next ch sp, ch 3**, cl shell in next cl shell, rep from * around, ending last rep at **, join.

Rnd 35: Sl st in beg cl shell, beg cl shell in same ch sp, *ch 3, (3 dc, ch 2, 3 dc) in ch sp of next shell, ch 3, cl shell in next cl shell, ch 3, sc in next ch sp, ch 5, sc in next ch-2 sp, [ch 2, sc in next ch-2 sp] 3 times, ch 5, sk next ch sp, sc in next ch sp, ch 3**, cl shell in next cl shell, rep from * around, ending last rep at **, join.

Rnd 36: Sl st in beg cl shell, beg cl shell in same ch sp, *ch 3, sk next sp, ({dc, ch 1} 5 times, dc) in next ch sp, ch 3, cl shell in next cl shell, ch 3, sc in next ch sp, ch 7, sc in next ch-2 sp, [ch 2, sc in next ch-2 sp] twice, ch 7, sk next ch sp, sc in next ch sp, ch 3**, cl shell in next cl shell, rep from * around, ending last rep at **, join.

Rnd 37: Sl st in beg cl shell, ch 4 *(counts as first dc, ch-1)*, ({dc, ch 1} 4 times, dc) in same ch sp, *ch 2, dc in next ch-1 sp, [ch 1, dc in next ch-1 sp] 4 times, ch 2, ({dc, ch 1} 5 times, dc) in next cl shell, ch 3, sc in next ch sp, ch 9, sc in next ch-2 sp, ch 2, sc in next ch-2 sp, ch 9, sk next ch sp, sc in next ch sp, ch 3**, ({dc, ch 1} 5 times, dc) in next cl shell, rep from * around, ending last rep at **, join with sl st in third ch of beg ch-4.

Rnd 38: Sl st in first ch-1 sp, ch 3, dc in same ch sp, *[ch 2, 2 dc in next ch sp] 4 times, ch 2, sc in center dc of next 5-dc group, ch 2, sk next 2 ch-1 sps and next ch-2 sp, 2 dc in next ch sp, [ch 2, 2 dc in next ch sp] 4 times, ch 3, sc in next ch sp, ch 9, sc in next ch-2 sp, ch 9, sk next ch sp, sc in next ch sp, ch 3**, 2 dc in next ch sp, rep from * around, ending last rep at **, join sl st in third ch of beg ch-3.

Rnd 39: Sl st in next dc and in ch-2 sp, beg dc cl in same ch sp, *[ch 3, dc cl in next ch sp] 10 times, ch 3, [3 sc in next ch-9 ch sp] twice, ch 3, dc cl in next ch sp, ch 3**, dc cl in next ch sp, rep from * around, ending last rep at **, join.

Rnd 40: Sl st in next sp, ch 1, (sc, ch 3, sc) in same ch sp, *[ch 2, (sc, ch 3, sc) in next sp] 10 times, ch 3, (sc, ch 3, sc) in fourth sc of next 6-sc group, ch 3, (sc, ch 3, sc) in next ch sp**, [ch 2, (sc, ch 3 sc) in next ch sp] twice, rep from * around, ending last rep at **, ch 2, (sc, ch 3, sc) in next ch sp, ch 2, join. Fasten off.❑❑

Pineapple Bathroom

Designs by Agnes Russell

SKILL LEVEL
■■■❑ INTERMEDIATE

FINISHED SIZES
Tank cover: 9 x 18 inches
Lid cover: 14 x 16 inches
Bathroom tissue cover: 4½ inches high
Air freshener doll: 9 inches tall
Wastebasket: 10½ inches high
Tissue box cover: 9½ inches long x 4¾ inches wide x 4¾ inches high
Curtain tiebacks: 20 inches long
Shower curtain valance: 9½ inches wide x 72 inches long

MATERIALS
❑ South Maid crochet cotton size 10 (350 yds per ball): 9 balls jade
❑ Size 8/1.50mm steel crochet hook or size needed to obtain gauge
❑ Tapestry needle

- Sewing needle
- Sewing thread
- Fibre-Craft Ariel air freshener doll
- 2 snap fasteners
- 1/3 yd 54-inch-wide white tulle
- 12 cream 19mm ribbon roses with stems
- 2½ yds white elastic cord
- 6 yds ¼-inch-wide cream ribbon
- 4 paper clips
- Spray starch
- White vanity wastebasket (10¼ long x 9¼ wide x 10½ inches high)
- 15 x 20 inches white poster board
- 16 plastic ½-inch rings
- Glue gun

GAUGE
3 shells = 1 inch
Take time to check gauge.

SPECIAL STITCHES
Beginning shell (beg shell): Sl st to ch sp, ch 3 *(counts as first dc)*, (dc, ch 2, 2 dc) in indicated st or ch sp.

Shell: (2 dc, ch 2, 2 dc) in indicated st or ch sp.

Beginning double shell (beg double shell): Sl st to ch sp, ch 3 *(counts as first dc)*, (dc, ch 2, 2 dc, ch 2, 2 dc) in indicated st or ch sp.

Double shell: (2 dc, ch 2, 2 dc, ch 2, 2 dc) in indicated st.

V-stitch (V-st): (Dc, ch 2, dc) in indicated st.

BATHROOM TISSUE COVER INSTRUCTIONS
Rnd 1 (RS): Ch 5, sl st in first ch to form ring, ch 3 *(counts as first dc)*, 11 dc in ring, join with sl st in top of beg ch-3. *(12 dc)*

Rnd 2: Ch 1, sc in first dc, ch 3, [sc in next dc, ch 3] around, join with sl st in beg sc. *(12 ch-3 sps)*

Rnd 3: Sl st into ch-3 sp, ch 1, sc in same ch-3 sp, ch 3, [sc in next ch-3 sp, ch 3] around, join

Rnd 4: Beg shell *(see Special Stitches)* in first ch-3 sp, **shell** *(see Special Stitches)* in each ch-3 sp around, join. *(12 shells)*

Rnd 5: Beg shell in shell, *ch 2, 6 dc in next shell, ch 2**, shell in shell, rep from * around, ending last rep at **, join.

Rnd 6: Beg shell in shell, *ch 2, dc in first dc of 6-dc group, [ch 1, dc in next dc] 5 times, ch 2**, shell in shell, rep from * around, ending last rep at **, join.

Rnd 7: Beg double shell *(see Special Stitches)* in shell, *ch 2, sc in next ch-1 sp, [ch 3, sc in next ch-1 sp] 4 times, ch 2**, **double shell** *(see Special Stitches)* in shell, rep from * around, ending last rep at **, join.

Rnd 8: Beg shell in shell, ch 1, shell in shell, *ch 2, sc in next ch-3 sp, [ch 3, sc in next ch-3 sp] 3 times, ch 2**, shell in shell, ch 1, shell in shell, rep from * around, ending last rep at **, join.

Rnd 9: Beg shell in shell, *ch 2, dc in ch-1 sp, ch 2, shell in shell, ch 2, sc in next ch-3 sp, [ch 3, sc in next ch-3 sp] twice, ch 2**, shell in shell, rep from * around, ending last rep at **, join.

Rnd 10: Beg shell in shell, *ch 2, **V-st** *(see Special Stitches)* in single dc, ch 2, shell in shell, ch 2, sc in next ch-3 sp, ch 3, sc in next ch-3 sp, ch 2**, shell in shell, rep from * around, ending last rep at **, join.

Rnd 11: Beg shell in shell, *ch 2, 6 dc in ch-2 sp of V-st, ch 2, shell in shell, ch 1, dc in ch-3 sp, ch 1**, shell in shell, rep from * around, ending last rep at **, join.

Rnd 12: Beg shell in shell, *ch 2, dc in first dc of 6-dc group, [ch 1, dc in next dc] 5 times, ch 2**, shell in each of next 2 shells, rep from * around, ending last rep at **, shell in shell, join.

Rnd 13: Beg shell in shell, *ch 2, sc in next ch-1 sp, [ch 3, sc in next ch-1 sp] 4 times, ch 2**, shell in each of next 2 shells, rep from * around, ending last rep at **, shell in shell, join.

Rnd 14: Beg shell, *ch 2, sc in next ch-3 sp, [ch 3, sc in next ch-3 sp] 3 times, ch 2, shell in shell, ch 1**, shell in shell, rep from * around, ending last rep at **, join.

Rnd 15: Beg shell in shell, *ch 2, sc in next ch-3 sp [ch 3, sc in next ch-3 sp] twice, ch 2, shell in shell, ch 2, dc in next ch-1 sp, ch 2**, shell in shell, rep from * around, ending last rep at **, join.

Rnd 16: Beg shell in shell, *ch 2, sc in next ch-3 sp, ch 3, sc in next ch-3 sp, ch 2, shell in shell, ch 2, V-st in single dc, ch 2** shell in shell, rep from * around, ending last rep at ** join.

Rnd 17: Beg shell in shell, *ch 1, dc in ch-3 sp, ch 1, shell in shell, ch 2, 6 dc in ch sp of V-st, ch 2**, shell in shell, rep from * around, ending last rep at **, join.

Rnd 18: Beg shell in shell, *shell in shell, ch 2, dc in first dc of 6-dc group, [ch 1, dc in next dc] 5 times, ch 2, shell in shell, rep from * around, turn.

Rnd 19: Beg shell in shell, *shell in shell, ch 2, sc in next ch-1 sp, [ch 3, sc in next ch-1 sp] 4 times, ch 2, shell in shell, rep from * around, join.

Rnds 20–28: Rep rnds 8–16.

Rnd 29: Beg shell in shell, *ch 1, dc in ch-3 sp, ch 1, shell in shell, ch 2, shell in ch-2 sp of V-st, ch 2**, shell in shell, rep from * around, ending last rep at **, join.

Rnd 30: Sl st in ch-2 sp, ch 1, sc in same ch sp, ch 3, sc in single dc at top of pineapple, [ch 3, sc in ch sp of next shell, ch 3, sc in next ch-2 sp] twice, ch 3, *sc in ch sp of next shell, ch 3, sc in next single dc at top of pineapple, [ch 3, sc in ch sp of next shell, ch 3, sc in next ch-2 sp] twice, ch 3, rep from * around, join with sl st in beg sc.

Rnd 31: Ch 1, 3 sc in each ch-3 sp around, join. Fasten off.

TIE
Ch 150. Fasten off.
Place cover over bathroom tissue. Weave ch through ch-3 sps of rnd 30, pull ends slightly to gather, tie ends in bow.

LID & TANK COVERS

Row 1 (WS): Ch 64, (dc, ch 2, 2 dc) in fourth ch from hook, [sk next 5 chs, **shell** (see Special Stitches) in next ch] 10 times, turn. *(11 shells)*

Row 2 (RS): Beg shell (see Special Stitches) in shell, [ch 2, 6 dc in next ch-2 sp of shell, ch 2, shell in shell] 5 times, turn.

Row 3: Beg shell in shell, *ch 2, dc in first dc of 6-dc group, [ch 1, dc in next dc] 5 times, ch 2, shell in shell, rep from * across, turn.

Row 4: Beg double shell (see Special Stitches) in shell, *ch 2, sc in next ch-1 sp, [ch 3, sc in next ch-1 sp] 4 times, ch 2, **double shell** (see Special Stitches) in shell, rep from * across, turn.

Row 5: Beg shell in shell, ch 1, shell in shell, *ch 2, sc in next ch-3 sp, [ch 3, sc in next ch-3 sp] 3 times, ch 2, shell in shell, ch 1, shell in shell, rep from * across, turn.

Row 6: Beg shell in shell, ch 1, dc in ch-1 sp, ch 1, shell in shell, *ch 2, sc in next ch-3 sp, [ch 3, sc in next ch-3 sp] twice, ch 2, shell in shell, ch 1, dc in next ch-1 sp, ch 1, shell in shell, rep from * across, turn.

Row 7: Beg shell in shell, ch 2, **V-st** (see Special Stitches) in single dc, ch 2, shell in shell, [ch 2, sc in next ch-3 sp, ch 3, sc in next ch-3 sp, ch 2, shell in shell, ch 2, V-st in single dc, ch 2, shell in shell] across, turn.

Row 8: Beg shell in shell, ch 2, 6 dc in ch-2 sp of V-st, ch 2, shell in shell, [ch 1, dc in next ch-3 sp, ch 1, shell in shell, ch 2, 6 dc in ch-2 sp of V-st, ch 2, shell in shell] across, turn.

Row 9: Beg shell in shell, *ch 2, dc in first dc of 6-dc group, [ch 1, dc in next dc] 5 times, ch 2**, shell in each of next 2 shells, rep from * across, ending last rep at **, shell in shell, turn.

Row 10: Beg shell in shell, *ch 2, sc in next ch-1 sp, [ch 3, sc in next ch-1 sp] 4 times, ch 2**, shell in each of next 2 shells, rep from * across, ending last rep at **, shell in shell, turn.

Row 11: Beg shell in shell, ch 2, sc in next ch-3 sp, [ch 3, sc in next ch-3 sp] 3 times, ch 2, shell in shell, *ch 1, shell in shell, ch 2, sc in next ch-3 sp, [ch 3, sc in next ch-3 sp] 3 times, ch 2, shell in shell, rep from * across, turn.

Row 12: Beg shell in shell, ch 2, sc in next ch-3 sp, [ch 3, sc in next ch-3 sp] twice, ch 2, shell in shell, *ch 1, dc in next ch-1 sp, ch 1, shell in shell, ch 2, sc in next ch-3 sp, [ch 3, sc in next ch-3 sp] twice, ch 2, shell in shell, rep from * across, turn.

Row 13: Beg shell in shell, ch 2, sc in next ch-3 sp, ch 3, sc in next ch-3 sp, ch 2, shell in shell, *ch 2, V-st in single dc, ch 2, shell in shell, ch 2, sc in next ch-3 sp, ch 3, sc in next ch-3 sp, ch 2, shell in shell, rep from * across, turn.

Row 14: Beg shell in shell, ch 1, dc in ch-3 sp, ch 1, shell in shell, *ch 2, 6 dc in ch-2 sp of V-st, ch 2, shell in shell, ch 1, dc in next ch-3 sp, ch 1, shell in shell, rep from * across, turn.

Row 15: Beg shell in shell, shell in shell, *ch 2, dc in first dc of 6-dc group, [ch 1, dc in next dc] 5 times, ch 2, shell in each of next 2 shells, rep from * across, turn.

Row 16: Beg shell in shell, shell in shell, *ch 2, sc in next ch-1 sp, [ch 3, sc in next ch-1 sp] 4 times, ch 2, shell in each of next 2 shells, rep from * across, turn.

Row 17: Beg shell in shell, ch 1, shell in shell, *ch 2, sc in next ch-3 sp, [ch 3, sc in next ch-3 sp] 3 times, ch 2, shell in shell, ch 1, shell in shell, rep from * across, turn.

Rows 18–29: Rep rows 6–17.

Rows 30–40: Rep rows 6–16.

Row 41: Sl st into ch-2 sp of shell, ch 3 only in this ch-2 sp of shell *(shell dec)*, *shell in shell, ch 2, sc in next ch-3 sp, [ch 3, sc in next ch-3 sp] 3 times, ch 2, shell in shell**, ch 1*, rep from * across, ending last rep at **, dc in ch-2 sp of last shell *(shell dec)*, turn.

Row 42: Sl st into ch-2 sp of last shell made, shell in shell, ch 2, sc in next ch-3 sp, [ch 3, sc in next ch-3 sp] twice, ch 2, shell in shell, *ch 1, dc in ch-1 sp, ch 1, shell in shell, ch 2, sc in next ch-3 sp, [ch 3, sc in next ch-3 sp] twice, ch 2, shell in shell, rep from * across, turn.

Row 43: Beg shell in shell, ch 2, sc in next ch-3 sp, ch 3, sc in next ch-3 sp, ch 2, shell in shell, *ch 2, V-st in single dc, ch 2, shell in shell, ch 2, sc in next ch-3 sp, ch 3, sc in next ch-3 sp, ch 2, shell in shell, rep from * across, turn.

Row 44: Beg shell in shell, ch 1, dc in ch-3 sp, ch 1, shell in shell, *ch 2, 6 dc in ch-2 sp of V-st, ch 2, shell in shell, ch 1, dc in ch-3 sp, ch 1, shell in shell, rep from * across, turn.

Row 45: Beg shell in shell, shell in shell, *ch 2, dc in first dc of 6-dc group, [ch 1, dc in next dc] 5 times, ch 2, shell in each of next 2 shells, rep from * across, turn.

Row 46: Beg shell in shell, shell in shell, *ch 2, sc in next ch-1 sp, [ch 3, sc in next ch-1 sp] 4 times, ch 2, shell in each of next 2 shells, rep from * across, turn.

Row 47: Sl st into ch-2 sp of shell, ch 3 only in this ch-2 sp of shell *(shell dec)*, shell in next shell, ch 2, sc in next ch-3 sp, [ch 3, sc in next ch-3 sp] 3 times, ch 2, shell in shell, *ch 1, shell in shell, ch 2, sc in next ch-3 sp, [ch 3, sc in next ch-3 sp] 3 times, ch 2, shell in shell*, rep between * twice, dc in ch-2 sp of last shell *(shell dec)*, turn.

Row 48: Sl st into ch-2 sp of last shell made, beg shell in shell, ch 2, sc in next ch-3 sp, [ch 3, sc in next ch-3 sp] twice, ch 2, shell in shell, *ch 1, dc in next ch-1 sp, ch 1, shell in shell, ch 2, sc in next ch-3 sp, [ch 3, sc in next ch-3 sp] twice, ch 2, shell in shell, rep from * across, turn.

Row 49: Beg shell in shell, ch 2, sc in next ch-3 sp, ch 3, sc in next ch-3 sp, ch 2, shell in shell, *ch 2, V-st in single dc, ch 2, shell in shell, ch 2, sc in next ch-3 sp, ch 3, sc in next ch-3 sp, ch 2, shell in shell, rep from * across, turn.

Row 50: Beg shell in shell, ch 1, dc in next ch-3 sp, ch 1, shell in shell, *ch 2, shell in ch-2 sp of V-st, ch 2, shell in shell, ch 1, dc in next ch-3 sp, ch 1, shell in shell, rep from * across, turn.

Row 51: Beg shell in shell, shell in shell, *ch 2, shell in shell, ch 2, [shell in shell] twice, rep from * twice. Fasten off.

TRIM
Rnd 1 (RS): Join with sl st in opposite side of starting ch, ch 1, sc in same ch as beg ch-1, [sc in each of next 5 chs, sc in next ch at base of shell] 10 times, continuing up left edge, [ch 3, sc in end of next row] 40 times, ch 3, sc in ch-3 sp of shell dec of row 41, ch 3, sk next dc, sc in end of row 41 just before ch-2 sp of shell, [ch 3, sc in end of next row] 5 times, ch 3, sc in ch-3 sp of dec shell of row 47, ch 3, sk next dc of row 47, sc in next dc just before ch-2 sp of shell, [ch 3, sc in end of next row] 4 times, working across top edge of row 51, [ch 3, sc in next ch-2 sp] 17 times, [ch 3, sc in end of next row] 4 times, working on row 47, ch 3, sc in next dc of shell, ch 3, sk next dc, sc in ch-3 of row 47 at dec shell, [ch 3, sc in end of next row] 5 times, working on row 41, ch 3, sc in next dc of shell, ch 3, sk next dc, sc in ch-3 of row 41 at dec shell, [ch 3, sc in end of next row] 40 times, ch 3, join with sl st in beg sc, **do not turn.**

Rnd 2: Ch 1, sc in each sc across back edge, sc in next ch-3 sp, ch 3, [sc in next ch-3 sp, ch 3] rep around, ending with sc in last ch-3 sp, join.

Rnd 3: Ch 1, sc in each sc across back edge, sc in next ch-3 sp, ch 4, [sc in next ch-3 sp, ch 4] around, ending with sc in last ch-3 sp, join.

Rnd 4: Ch 1, sc in each sc across back edge, ch 4, [sc in next ch-4 sp, ch 4] rep around, join with sl st in beg sc.

Note: *Cut 26-inch length elastic cord; tie ends in a knot to form a 25-inch elastic cord circle.*

Rnd 5: Working over elastic cord circle *(see Illustration)* and ch-4 sps, position knot at center back edge, ch 1, 5 sc over cord in each ch-4 sp around, join. Fasten off.

Sc Over Elastic

AIR FRESHENER DOLL
HAT
Brim
Rnd 1 (RS): Ch 60, sl st in first ch to form ring, **beg double shell** *(see Special Stitches)* in first ch, ch 2, sk next 4 chs, 6 dc in next ch, ch 2, sk next 4 chs, [**double shell** *(see Special Stitches)* in next ch, ch 2, sk next 4 chs, 6 dc in next ch, ch 2, sk next 4 chs] 5 times, join with sl st in top of beg ch-3.

Rnd 2: Beg shell *(see Special Stitches)* in shell, ***shell** *(see Special Stitches)* in shell, ch 2, dc in first dc of 6-dc group, [ch 1, dc in next dc] 5 times, ch 2**, shell in shell, rep from * around, ending last rep at **, join.

Rnd 3: Beg shell in shell, *shell in shell, ch 2, sc in next ch-1 sp, [ch 3, sc in next ch-1 sp] 4 times, ch 2**, shell in shell, rep from * around, ending last rep at **, join.

Rnd 4: Beg shell in shell, *shell in shell, ch 2, sc in next ch-3 sp, [ch 3, sc in next ch-3 sp] 3 times, ch 2**, shell in shell, rep from * around, ending last rep at **, join.

Rnd 5: Beg shell in shell, *ch 3, sc in sp between 2 shells directly below, ch 3, shell in shell, ch 2, sc in next ch-3 sp, [ch 3, sc in next ch-3 sp] twice, ch 2**, shell in shell, rep from * around, ending last rep at **, join.

Rnd 6: Beg shell in shell, *ch 3, [sc in next ch-3 sp, ch 3] twice, shell in shell, ch 2, sc in next ch-3 sp, ch 3, sc in next ch-3 sp, ch 2**, shell in shell, rep from * around, ending last rep at **, join.

Rnd 7: Sl st into ch-2 sp of shell, ch 1, *[sc, ch 3] 3 times in ch-2 sp of shell, sc in same ch sp, (sc, ch 3, sc) in each of next 3 ch-3 sps, [sc, ch 3] 3 times in ch-2 sp of next shell, sc in same ch sp, ch 4, (sc, ch 3, sc) in ch-3 sp of pineapple, ch 4, rep from * around, join with sl st in beg sc. Fasten off.

Rnd 8: Join with sl st in opposite side of starting ch of rnd 1 in ch-4 sp of brim, ch 1, working in sk ch-4 sps only, work 5 sc in each ch-4 sp, join. *(60 sc)*

Rnd 9: Ch 4 *(counts as first dc and ch-1)*, sk next sc, [dc in next sc, ch 1, sk next sc] around, join with sl st in third ch of beg ch-4. *(30 ch-1 sps)*

Rnd 10: Ch 1, sc in first st, sc in next ch-1 sp, [sc in next dc, sc in next ch-1 sp] around, join. Fasten off. *(60 sc)*

Crown
Rnd 1: Ch 5, sl st in first ch to form ring, ch 3 *(counts as first dc)*, 14 dc in ring, join with sl st in top of beg ch-3. *(15 dc)*

Rnd 2: Ch 3, dc in same st, 2 dc in each dc around, join. *(30 dc)*

Rnd 3: Ch 1, sc in first st, 2 sc in next dc, [sc in next dc, 2 sc in next dc] around, join. *(45 sc)*

Rnd 4: Ch 1, sc in first sc, sc in next sc, 2 sc in next sc, [sc in each of next 2 sc, 2 sc in next sc] around, join. *(60 sc)*

Rnd 5: With WS tog, holding rnd 4 of crown to rnd 10 of Brim, ch 1, working through both thicknesses, sl st in each st around. Fasten off.

FINISHING
1. Cut a 24-inch length of cream ribbon. Weave ribbon through rnd 9 of Brim over 2 dc, under 2 dc around; tie ends in a bow. With sewing needle and thread, tack knot of bow to secure.
2. Cut stems from six ribbon roses. With glue gun, glue roses over each group of 2-dc of rnd 9 visible from weaving ribbon.
3. Place Hat on a flat surface, press Brim and spray with starch. Allow to dry completely.
4. Holding doll, gather top and sides of hair at back; separate into three groups; braid hair. Tie a 7-inch length of cream ribbon in a bow around the end of braid.
5. Secure Hat to head with paper clips.

DRESS
Skirt
Row 1: Starting at waistline, ch 84, dc, ch 2, 2 dc in fourth ch from hook, ch 2, sk next 4 chs, 6 dc in next ch, ch 2, sk next 4 chs, [shell in next ch, ch 2, sk next 4 chs, 6 dc in next ch, ch 2, sk 4 chs] 7 times, shell in last ch, turn.

Row 2: Beg shell in shell, *ch 2, dc in first dc of 6-dc group, [ch 1, dc in next dc] 5 times, ch 2, shell in shell, rep from * across, turn.

Row 3: Beg shell in shell, *ch 2, sc in next ch-1 sp, [ch 3, sc in next ch-1 sp] 4 times, ch 2**, double shell in shell, rep from * around, ending last rep at **, shell in shell, turn.

Note: Beg with rnd 4, at the end of each rnd, join with sl st in third ch of beg ch-3, sl st into ch-2 sp of that joining shell, turn.

Rnd 4: Beg shell in shell, *ch 2, sc in next ch-3 sp, [ch 3, sc in next ch-3 sp] 3 times, ch 2, shell in shell, ch 1**, shell in shell, rep from * around, ending last rep at **, join *(see Note)*.

Rnd 5: Beg shell in shell, ch 1, dc in ch-1 sp, ch 1, shell in shell, ch 2, sc in next ch-3 sp, [ch 3, sc in next ch-3 sp] twice, ch 2**, shell in shell, rep from * around, ending last rep at **, join.

Rnd 6: Beg shell in shell, *ch 2, sc in next ch-3 sp, ch 3, sc in next ch-3 sp, ch 2, shell in shell, ch 2, V-st in single dc, ch 2**, shell in shell, rep from * around, ending last rep at **, join.

Rnd 7: Beg shell in shell, *ch 2, 6 dc in ch-2 sp of V-st, ch 2, shell in shell, ch 1, dc in rem ch-3 sp, ch 1**, shell in shell, rep from * around, ending last rep at **, join.

Rnd 8: Beg shell in shell, *shell in shell, ch 2, dc in first dc of 6-dc group, [ch 1, dc in next dc] 5 times, ch 2**, shell in shell, rep from * around, ending last rep at **, join.

Rnd 9: Beg shell in shell, *ch 2, sc in next ch-1 sp, [ch 3, sc in next ch-1 sp] 4 times, ch 2*, shell in each of next 2 shells, rep from * around, ending last rep at **, shell in shell, join.

Rnd 10: Beg shell in shell, *ch 1, shell in shell, ch 2, sc in next ch-3 sp, [ch 3, sc in next ch-3 sp] 3 times, ch 2, shell in shell, rep from * around, ch 1, join.

Rnd 11: Beg shell in shell, *ch 2, sc in next ch-3 sp, [ch 3, sc in next ch-3 sp] twice, ch 2, shell in shell, ch 1, dc in next ch-1 sp, ch 1**, shell in shell, rep from * around, ending last rep at **, join.

Rnd 12: Beg shell in shell, *ch 2, V-st in single dc, ch 2, shell in shell, ch 2, sc in next ch-3 sp, ch 3, sc in next ch-3 sp, ch 2**, shell in shell, rep from * around, ending last rep at **, join.

Rnd 13: Beg shell in shell, *ch 1, dc in next ch-3 sp, ch 1, shell in shell, ch 2, 6 dc in ch-2 sp of V-st, ch 2**, shell in shell, rep from * around, ending last rep at **, join.

Rnd 14: Beg shell in shell, *ch 2, dc in first dc of 6-dc group, [ch 1, dc in next dc] 5 times, ch 2**, shell in each of next 2 shells, rep from * around, ending last rep at **, shell in shell, join.

Rnd 15: Beg shell in shell, *shell in shell, ch 2, sc in next ch-1 sp, [ch 3, sc in next ch-1 sp] 4 times, ch 2, shell in shell, rep from * around, join.

Rnd 16: Beg shell in shell, ch 1, *shell in shell, ch 2, sc in next ch-3 sp, [ch 3, sc in next ch-3 sp] 3 times, ch 2, shell in shell, ch 1, rep from * around, join.

Rnd 17: Beg shell in shell, *ch 3, sc in next ch-1 sp, ch 3, shell in shell, ch 2, sc in next ch-3 sp, [ch 3, sc in next ch-3 sp] twice, ch 2**, shell in shell, rep from * around, ending last rep at **, join.

Rnd 18: Beg shell in shell, *ch 2, sc in next ch-3 sp, ch 3, sc in next ch-3 sp, ch 2, shell in shell, [ch 3, sc in next ch-3 sp] twice, ch 3**, shell in shell, rep from * around, ending last rep at **, join.

Rnd 19: Ch 1, *(2 sc, ch 3, 2 sc) in ch-2 sp of shell, [(2 sc, ch 3, 2 sc) in next ch-3 sp] 3 times, (2 sc, ch 3, 2 sc) in next ch-2 sp of shell, ch 3, (sc, ch 3, sc) in rem ch-3 sp of pineapple, ch 3, rep from * around, join with sl st in beg sc. Fasten off.

Waistband Beading
Row 1: Join with sl st in starting ch on opposite side of row 1 of Skirt, ch 4 *(counts as first dc and ch-1)*, sk next 4 chs, dc in next ch, [ch 1, sk next 4 chs, dc in next ch] 15 times, turn. *(17 dc)*

Bodice
Row 2: Ch 1, sc in first dc, sc in next ch-1 sp, [sc in next dc, sc in next ch-1 sp] 15 times, do not sc in last dc, turn. *(32 sc)*

Row 3: Ch 1, sc in each sc across, turn.
Row 4: Ch 1, sc in each of first 14 sc, ch 1, sk next sc, sc in each of next 2 sc, ch 1, sk next sc, sc in each of last 14 sc, turn.
Row 5: Ch 1, sc in each of first 14 sc, [ch 3, sc in next ch-1 sp] twice, ch 3, sc in each of last 14 sc, turn.
Row 6: Ch 1, sc in each of first 14 sc, [ch 3, sc in next ch-3 sp] 3 times, ch 3, sc in each of last 14 sc, turn.
Row 7: Ch 1, sc in each of first 11 sc, [ch 3, sc in next ch-3 sp] 4 times, ch 3, sk next 3 sc, sc in each of last 11 sc, turn.

Right Back
Row 8: Ch 1, sc in each of next 6 sc, turn. *(6 sc)*
Rows 9–14: Ch 1, sc in each of next 6 sc, turn. At the end of last row, fasten off.

Left Back
Row 8: With WS facing, join with sl st in sixth sc of row 7 from edge, ch 1, sc in same sc as beg ch-1, sc in each of next 5 sc, turn. *(6 sc)*
Rows 9–14: Ch 1, sc in each of next 6 sc, turn. At the end of last row, fasten off.

Front
Row 8: Join with sl st in first ch-3 sp of row 7 on front, ch 1, 3 sc in same ch-3 sp, 3 sc in each of next 4 ch-3 sps, turn. *(15 sc)*
Rows 9 & 10: Ch 1, sc in each 15 sc across, turn.

Right Shoulder Shaping
Row 11: Ch 1, sc in each of next 6 sc, turn. *(6 sc)*
Rows 12–14: Ch 1, sc in each of next 6 sc, turn.
Row 15: Holding row 14 of front right shoulder and Back Right tog, matching sts, sl st across 6 sts. Fasten off.

Left Shoulder Shaping
Row 11: With WS facing, join with sl st in sixth sc of row 10 from edge, ch 1, sc in same sc, sc in each of next 5 sc, turn. *(6 sc)*
Rows 12–14: Ch 1, sc in each of next 6 sc, turn.
Row 15: Holding row 14 of Front Left Shoulder Shaping and Back Left tog, matching sts, sl st across 6 sts. Fasten off.

Neckline Trim
Row 1 (RS): Join with sl st in end of row 1 of Waistband Beading, ch 1, 3 sc in end of row 1, sc in next sc, [ch 2, sk next st, sc in next st] around to within opposite edge of row 1 of Waistband Beading, 3 sc in end of row 1. Fasten off.
Row 2: Join with sl st in first ch-2 sp of row 1, ch 1, (sc, ch 2, sc) in ch-2 sp, (sc, ch 2, sc) in each ch-2 sp across. Fasten off.

Sleeves
Rnd 1: Join with sl st at underarm, ch 1, sc in same st, ch 2, evenly sp [sc, ch 2] 10 times around armhole opening, join with sl st in beg sc.
Rnds 2–4: Sl st into ch-2 sp, ch 1, sc in same ch-2 sp, ch 2, [sc in next ch-2 sp, ch 2] around, join.
Rnd 5: Sl st into ch-2 sp, ch 1, (sc, ch 2, sc) in same ch-2 sp, (sc, ch 2, sc) in each ch-2 sp around, join. Fasten off.

Starch and press dress.
Sew a snap fastener at back opening over 3 sc of row 1 of Neckline Trim.
Cut 24-inch length of cream ribbon. Starting at center front, weave through ch-1 sps of Waistline Beading around, ending at center front. Place Dress on doll; tie ends in a bow at center front. Trim ends at a slight angle.

SLIP
1. Fold the 12 x 54-inch piece of tulle in half to measure 6 x 54 inches.
2. Thread sewing needle with double length of sewing thread.
3. Working across folded edge ⅛ inch from edge, work running stitch across edge; pull gently to gather to measure 5½ inches across gathered edge; knot to secure.
4. With opening at back, sew a snap fastener at edge of gathered section. Place on doll with snap at back.

BOUQUET
Wind stems of six rem ribbon roses one at a time around tapestry needle to curl. Gather roses into a bouquet. Tie a 7-inch length of ribbon around base of roses; knot to secure. Trim ends at a slight angle. With glue gun, glue bouquet to right palm of doll.

WASTEBASKET COVER
Rnd 1 (RS): Starting at top of basket, leaving a 3-inch length at beg, ch 237, **shell** *(see Special Stitches)* in fourth ch from hook, [sk next 5 chs, shell in next ch] 38 times, 5 chs rem, with care not to twist, join with sl st in third ch of beg fourth ch. *(39 shells)*
Note: *Join beg 3-inch length in base of first shell of rnd 1.*
Rnd 2: Beg shell *(see Special Stitches)* in shell, *shell in shell twice, ch 2, 6 dc in next shell, ch 2, shell in shell, rep from * around, join. *(13 pineapple bases; 26 shells)*
Rnd 3: Beg shell in shell, *shell in shell, ch 2, dc in first dc of 6-dc group, [ch 1, dc in next dc] 5 times, ch 2, shell in shell, rep from * around, join.
Rnd 4: Beg shell in shell, *shell in shell, ch 2, sc in next ch-1 sp, [ch 3, sc in next ch-1 sp] 4 times, ch 2, shell in shell, rep from * around, join.
Rnd 5: Beg shell in shell, *ch 1, shell in shell, ch 2, sc in next ch-3

sp, [ch 3, sc in next ch-3 sp] 3 times, ch 2, shell in shell, rep from * around, ch 1, join.

Rnd 6: Beg shell in shell, *ch 2, dc in ch-1 sp, ch 2, shell in shell, ch 2, sc in next ch-3 sp, [ch 3, sc in next ch-3 sp] twice, ch 2**, shell in shell, rep from * around, ending last rep at **, join.

Rnd 7: Beg shell in shell, *ch 2, **V-st** *(see Special Stitches)* in single dc, ch 2, shell in shell, ch 2, sc in next ch-3 sp, ch 3, sc in next ch-3 sp, ch 2**, shell in shell, rep from * around, ending last rep at **, join.

Rnd 8: Beg shell in shell, *ch 2, 6 dc in ch-2 sp of V-st, ch 2, shell in shell, ch 1, dc in next ch-3 sp, ch 1**, shell in shell, rep from * around, ending last rep at **, join.

Rnd 9: Beg shell in shell, *ch 2, dc in first dc of 6-dc group, [ch 1, dc in next dc] 5 times, ch 2**, shell in each of next 2 shells, rep from * around, ending last rep at **, shell in shell, join.

Rnd 10: Beg shell in shell, *ch 2, sc in next ch-1 sp, [ch 3, sc in next ch-1 sp] 4 times, ch 2**, shell in each of next 2 shells, rep from * around, ending last rep at **, shell in shell, join.

Rnd 11: Beg shell in shell, *ch 2, sc in next ch-3 sp, [ch 3, sc in next ch-3 sp] 3 times, ch 2, shell in shell, ch 1**, shell in shell, rep from * around, ending last rep at **, join.

Note: *Because the wastebasket base is smaller, you will notice a slight change in pattern. The number of chs between shells and pineapples will decrease slightly without changing the pineapple size.*

Rnd 12: Beg shell in shell, *ch 2, sc in next ch-3 sp, [ch 3, sc in next ch-3 sp] twice, ch 2, shell in shell, ch 1, dc in next ch-1 sp, ch 1**, shell in shell, rep from * around, ending last rep at **, join.

Rnd 13: Beg shell in shell, *ch 2, sc in next ch-3 sp, ch 3, sc in next ch-3 sp, ch 2, shell in shell, ch 1, V-st in single dc, ch 1**, shell in shell, rep from * around, ending last rep at **, join.

Rnd 14: Beg shell in shell, *ch 1, dc in next ch-3 sp, ch 1, shell in shell, ch 1, 6 dc in ch-2 sp of V-st, ch 1**, shell in shell, rep from * around, ending last rep at **, join.

Rnd 15: Beg shell in shell, *shell in shell, ch 1, dc in first dc of 6-dc group, [ch 1, dc in next dc] 5 times, ch 1, shell in shell, rep from * around, join.

Rnd 16: Beg shell in shell, *shell in shell, ch 1, sk next ch-1 sp, sc in next ch-1 sp, [ch 3, sc in next ch-1 sp] 4 times, ch 1**, shell in shell, rep from * around, ending last rep at **, join.

Rnd 17: Beg shell in shell, ch 1, *shell in shell, sc in next ch-3 sp, [ch 3, sc in next ch-3 sp] 3 times, ch 1, shell in shell, ch 1, rep from * around, join.

Rnd 18: Beg shell in shell, *ch 1, dc in ch-1 sp, ch 1, shell in shell, ch 1, sc in next ch-3 sp, [ch 3, sc in next ch-3 sp] twice, ch 1**, shell in shell, rep from * around, ending last rep at **, join.

Rnd 19: Beg shell in shell, *ch 1, V-st in single dc, ch 1, shell in shell, ch 1, sc in next ch-3 sp, ch 3, sc in next ch-3 sp, ch 1**, shell in shell, rep from * around, ending last rep at **, join.

Rnd 20: Beg shell in shell, *ch 1, 6 dc in ch-2 sp of V-st, ch 1, shell in shell, ch 1, dc in next ch-3 sp, ch 1**, shell in shell, rep from * around, ending last rep at **, join.

Rnd 21: Beg shell in shell, *ch 1, dc in first dc of 6-dc group, [ch 1, dc in next dc] 5 times, ch 1**, shell in each of next 2 shells, rep from * around, ending last rep at **, shell in shell, join.

Rnd 22: Beg shell in shell, *ch 1, sk next ch-1 sp, sc in next ch-1 sp, [ch 3, sc in next ch-1 sp] 4 times, ch 1**, shell in each of next 2 shells, rep from * around, ending last rep at **, join.

Rnd 23: Beg shell in shell, *ch 1, sc in next ch-3 sp, [ch 3, sc in next ch-3 sp] 3 times, ch 1**, shell in shell, rep from * around, ending last rep at **, join.

Rnd 24: Beg shell in shell, *ch 1, sc in next ch-3 sp, [ch 3, sc in next ch-3 sp] twice, ch 1, shell in shell, ch 1, dc in ch-1 sp, ch 1**, shell in shell, rep from * around, ending last rep at **, join.

Rnd 25: Beg shell in shell, *ch 1, sc in next ch-3 sp, ch 3, sc in next ch-3 sp, ch 1, shell in shell, ch 1, V-st in single dc, ch 1**, shell in shell, rep from * around, ending last rep at **, join.

Rnd 26: Beg shell in shell, *dc in next ch-3 sp, shell in shell, ch 1, 6 dc in next V-st, ch 1**, shell in shell, rep from * around, ending last rep at **, join.

Rnd 27: Beg shell in shell, *shell in shell, ch 1, dc in first dc of 6-dc group, [ch 1, dc in next dc] 5 times, ch 1, shell in shell, rep from * around, join.

Rnd 28: Beg shell in shell, *shell in shell, ch 1, sk next ch-1 sp, sc in next ch-1 sp, [ch 3, sc in next ch-1 sp] 4 times, ch 1, shell in shell, rep from * around, join.

Rnd 29: Beg shell in shell, ch 1, *shell in shell, ch 1, sc in next ch-3 sp, [ch 3, sc in next ch-3 sp] 3 times, ch 1, shell in shell, ch 1, rep from * around, join.

Rnd 30: Beg shell in shell, *ch 1, sc in ch-1 sp, ch 1, shell in shell, ch 1, sc in next ch-3 sp, [ch 3, sc in next ch-3 sp] twice, ch 1**, shell in shell, rep from * around, ending last rep at **, join.

Rnd 31: Beg shell in shell, *ch 1, sc in next sc, ch 1, shell in shell, ch 1, sc in next ch-3 sp, ch 3, sc in next ch-3 sp, ch 1**, shell in shell, rep from * around, ending last rep at **, join.

Rnd 32: Beg shell in shell, *dc in sc, shell in shell, dc in next ch-3 sp**, shell in shell, rep from * around, ending last rep at **, join.

Rnd 33: Sl st into ch-2 sp of shell, ch 1, [sc in ch-2 sp of shell, ch 3, sc in single dc between shells, ch 3] around, join with sl st in beg sc. Fasten off.

TOP TRIM
Note: *Cut a 20-inch length of elastic cord; knot ends tog to form an 18-inch circle. Set aside.*

Rnd 1 (RS): Join with sl st in opposite side of starting ch in same ch as shell, ch 3, sl st in next ch-5 sp, ch 3, [sl st in same ch as shell, ch 3, sl st in next ch-5 sp, ch 3] around, ending with sl st in same ch as beg ch-3.

Rnds 2 & 3: Sl st into ch-3 sp, ch 3, [sl st in next ch-3 sp, ch 3] around, join with sl st in same st as beg ch-3.

Rnd 4: Working over elastic cord circle *(see illustration on page 45)* and into ch-3 sps, ch 1, 3 sc in each ch-3 sp around, join.

Rnd 5: Ch 4, sk next 2 sc, [sl st in next sc, ch 4, sk next 2 sc] around, join. Fasten off.

Cut a 36-inch length of cream ribbon; weave over and under shells of rnd 1 of Wastebasket Cover. Tie ends in a bow at center front; trim ends.

Place cover over wastebasket.

TISSUE BOX COVER

Rnd 1 (RS): Starting at center top, leaving a 3-inch length at beg, ch 195, **shell** *(see Special Stitches)* in fourth ch from hook, [sk next 5 chs, shell in next ch] 31 times, sk 5 chs, join. *(32 shells)*

Note: Join beg 3-inch length in base of first shell of rnd 1.

Rnd 2: Beg double shell *(see Special Stitches)* in shell, *ch 2, shell in shell, ch 2, [shell in shell] twice, ch 2, shell in shell, ch 2, **double shell** *(see Special Stitches)* in shell, [ch 2, shell in shell, ch 2, shell in each of next 2 shells] 3 times, ch 2, shell in shell, ch 2*, double shell in shell, rep between *, join.

Rnd 3: Beg shell in shell, *shell in shell, ch 2, 6 dc in next shell, ch 2, shell in shell, rep from * around, join. *(24 shells, 12 pineapple bases)*

Rnd 4: Beg shell in shell, *shell in shell, ch 2, dc in first dc of 6-dc group, [ch 1, dc in next dc] 5 times, ch 2, shell in shell, rep from * around, join.

Rnd 5: Beg shell in shell, *shell in shell, ch 2, sc in next ch-1 sp, [ch 3, sc in next ch-1 sp] 4 times, ch 2, shell in shell, rep from * around, join.

Rnd 6: Beg shell in shell, ch 1,*shell in shell, ch 2, sc in next ch-3 sp, [ch 3, sc in next ch-3 sp] 3 times, ch 2, shell in shell, ch 1, rep from * around, join.

Rnd 7: Beg shell in shell, *ch 2, dc in ch-1 sp, ch 2, shell in shell, ch 2, sc in next ch-3 sp, [ch 3, sc in next ch-3 sp] twice, ch 2**, shell in shell, rep from * around, ending last rep at **, join.

Rnd 8: Beg shell in shell, *ch 2, **V-st** *(see Special Stitches)* in single dc, ch 2, shell in shell, ch 2, sc in next ch-3 sp, ch 3, sc in next ch-3 sp, ch 2**, shell in shell, rep from * around, ending last rep at **, join.

Rnd 9: Beg shell in shell, *ch 2, 6 dc in V-st, ch 2, shell in shell, ch 1, dc in next ch-3 sp, ch 1**, shell in shell, rep from * around, ending last rep at **, join.

Rnd 10: Beg shell in shell, *ch 2, dc in first dc of 6-dc group, [ch 1, dc in next dc] 5 times, ch 2**, shell in each of next 2 shells, rep from * around, ending last rep at **, shell in shell, join.

Rnd 11: Beg shell in shell, *ch 2, sc in next ch-1 sp, [ch 3, sc in next ch-1 sp] 4 times, ch 2**, shell in each of next 2 shells, rep from * around, ending last rep at **, shell in shell, join.

Rnd 12: Beg shell in shell, *ch 2, sc in next ch-3 sp, [ch 3, sc in next ch-3 sp] 3 times, ch 2, shell in shell, ch 1**, shell in shell, rep from * around, ending last rep at **, join.

Rnd 13: Beg shell in shell, *ch 2, sc in next ch-3 sp, [ch 3, sc in next ch-3 sp] twice, ch 2, shell in shell, ch 2, dc in ch-1 sp, ch 2**, shell in shell, rep from * around, ending last rep at **, join.

Rnd 14: Beg shell in shell, *ch 2, sc in next ch-3 sp, ch 3, sc in next ch-3 sp, ch 2, shell in shell, ch 2, V-st in single dc, ch 2**, shell in shell, rep from * around, ending last rep at **, join.

Rnd 15: Beg shell in shell, *ch 1, dc in next ch-3 sp, ch 1, shell in shell, ch 2, 6 dc in V-st, ch 2**, shell in shell, rep from * around, ending last rep at **, join.

Rnds 16–20: Rep rnds 4–8.

Rnd 21: Beg shell in shell, *ch 2, shell in V-st, ch 2, shell in shell, ch 1, dc in next ch-3 sp, ch 1**, shell in shell, rep from * around, ending last rep at **, join.

Rnd 22: Sl st into ch-2 sp of shell, ch 1, *[sc in ch-2 sp of shell, ch 2, sc in ch-2 sp, ch 2] twice, sc in ch-2 sp of shell, ch 2, sc in single dc, ch 2, rep from * around, join with sl st in beg sc.

Note: Cut a 20-inch length of elastic cord; knot ends tog to form an 18-inch ring.

Rnd 23: Working over elastic cord

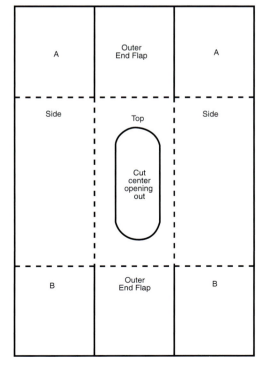

KEY
— Cut line
---- Fold line

(see illustration on page 45) and into ch-2 sps of rnd 22, ch 1, 3 sc in each ch-2 sp around, join. Fasten off.

TRIM
Rnd 1: Join with sl st in opposite side of starting ch of rnd 1 in base of any shell, [ch 4, sk next 5 chs, sl st in next ch at base of shell] around.
Rnd 2: Sl st into ch-4 sp, [ch 3, sl st in next ch-4 sp] around.
Rnd 3: Sl st into next ch-3 sp, [ch 3, sl st in next ch-3 sp] around.
Rnd 4: Sl st into next ch-3 sp, ch 1, (3 sc, ch 2, 3 sc) in each ch-3 sp around, join with sl st in beg sc. Fasten off.

Cut 34-inch length of cream ribbon. Starting on side edge, weave through ch sps created by rnd 1 of Tissue Box Cover and rnd 1 of Trim. Tie ends in a bow.

POSTER BOARD FORM
Note: *The poster board form is optional; however, most tissue boxes have designs or floral prints on them that will detract from the pineapple design.*

Using tissue box as a pattern and illustration as a guide, cut and fold poster board. With outer end flap on outside, glue A to A on top of one another. Glue outer end flap onto A. Rep on opposite end with the two sections of B and outer end flap.

Place form over tissue box. Place crocheted cover over tissue box form.

CURTAIN TIEBACKS
Make 2.
Rnd 1: Join with sl st to plastic ring, ch 1, 24 sc over ring, join in beg sc. *(24 sc)*
Row 2: Beg shell (*see Special Stitches*) in first st, [ch 2, sk next sc, **shell** (*see Special Stitches*) in next sc] twice, turn.
Row 3: Ch 3, shell in shell, ch 2, 6 dc in next shell, ch 2, shell in shell, turn.
Row 4: Ch 3, shell in shell, ch 2, dc in first dc of 6-dc group, [ch 1, dc in next dc] 5 times, ch 2, shell in shell, turn.
Row 5: Ch 3, shell in shell, ch 2, sc in next ch-1 sp, [ch 3, sc in next ch-1 sp] 4 times, ch 2, shell in shell, turn.
Row 6: Ch 3, shell in shell, ch 2, sc in next ch-3 sp, [ch 3, sc in next ch-3 sp] 3 times, ch 2, shell in shell, turn.
Row 7: Ch 3, shell in shell, ch 2, sc in next ch-3 sp, [ch 3, sc in next ch-3 sp] twice, ch 2, shell in shell, turn.
Row 8: Ch 3, shell in shell, ch 2, sc in next ch-3 sp, ch 3, sc in next ch-3 sp, ch 2, shell in shell, turn.
Row 9: Ch 3, shell in shell, ch 1, dc in next ch-3 sp, ch 1, shell in shell, turn.
Row 10: Ch 3, [shell in shell] twice, turn.
Row 11: Rep row 10.
Row 12: Ch 3, shell in shell, ch 1, shell in shell, turn.
Row 13: Ch 3, shell in shell, ch 1, dc in ch-1 sp, ch 1, shell in shell, turn.
Row 14: Ch 3, shell in shell, ch 1, **V-st** (*see Special Stitches*) in single dc, ch 1, shell in shell, turn.
Row 15: Ch 3, shell in shell, ch 2, 6 dc in V-st, ch 2, shell in shell, turn.
Rows 16–51: [Rep rows 4–15] 3 times.
Note: *If longer tiebacks are desired, rep rows 4–15 for each additional pineapple.*
Rows 52–59: Rep rows 4–11.
Row 60: Sl st into ch-2 sp of shell, ch 1, working over another plastic ring and into ch-2 sp of shell, work 3 sc, 3 sc over ring only, 3 sc over ring and next ch-2 sp of shell, work 15 sc over ring only, join with sl st in beg sc. Fasten off. *(24 sc over ring)*

SHOWER CURTAIN VALANCE
Notes: *Due to width of valance and a beg ch length of 583 chs to complete a total of 98 shells, it is much easier to work with two balls of thread.*

If you choose to work with only one ball, work a beg ch of 586 and beg in fourth ch from hook.

Row 1: With first ball start making foundation ch until several feet in length, draw up a lp, remove hook; attach second ball in first ch of foundation ch, **beg shell** (*see Special Stitches*) in first ch, *[sk next 5 chs, **shell** (*see Special Stitches*) in next ch] rep across ch length, when foundation ch length is worked, draw up a lp, remove hook, pick up dropped lp of first ball, continue making ch length for foundation, draw up a lp, remove hook, pick up ch lp from second ball, rep from * across until a total of 98 shells are completed, gently pull out any excess foundation ch on first ball to last shell; continuing with first ball and working across opposite side of foundation ch, ch 1, sc in same ch as last shell, [ch 4, sc in ch-5 sp, ch 4, sc in same ch as next shell] rep across foundation ch, turn. Fasten off first ball only.
Row 2: Pick up dropped lp from second ball, beg shell in shell, shell in shell *ch 2, 6 dc in next shell, ch 2, [shell in shell] twice, rep from * across, turn. *(32 pineapple bases; 66 shells)*
Row 3: Beg shell in shell, shell in shell, *ch 2, dc in first dc of 6-dc group, [ch 1, dc in next dc] 5 times, ch 2, shell in each of next

2 shells, rep from * across, turn.

Row 4: Beg shell in shell, shell in shell, *ch 2, sc in next ch-1 sp, [ch 3, sc in next ch-1 sp] 4 times, ch 2, shell in each of next 2 shells, rep from * across, turn.

Row 5: Beg shell in shell, ch 1, shell in shell, *ch 2, sc in next ch-3 sp, [ch 3, sc in next ch-3 sp] 3 times, ch 2, shell in shell, ch 1, shell in shell, rep from * across, turn.

Row 6: Beg shell in shell, ch 2, dc in ch-1 sp, ch 2, shell in shell, *ch 2, sc in next ch-3 sp, [ch 3, sc in next ch-3 sp] twice, ch 2, shell in shell, ch 2, dc in ch-1 sp, ch 2, shell in shell, rep from * across, turn.

Row 7: Beg shell in shell, ch 2, **V-st** (see Special Stitches) in single dc, *ch 2, sc in next ch-3 sp, ch 3, sc in next ch-3 sp, ch 2, shell in shell, ch 2, V-st in single dc, ch 2, shell in shell, rep from * across, turn.

Row 8: Beg shell in shell, ch 2, 6 dc in V-st, ch 2, shell in shell, *ch 1, dc in next ch-3 sp, ch 1, shell in shell, ch 2, 6 dc in V-st, ch 2, shell in shell, rep from * across, turn.

Row 9: Beg shell in shell, ch 2, dc in first dc of 6-dc group, [ch 1, dc in next dc] 5 times, ch 2, shell in shell, *shell in shell, ch 2, dc in first dc of 6-dc group, [ch 1, dc in next dc] 5 times, ch 2, shell in shell, rep from * across, turn.

Row 10: Beg shell in shell, ch 2, sc in next ch-1 sp, [ch 3, sc in next ch-1 sp] 4 times, ch 2, shell in shell, *shell in shell, ch 2, sc in next ch-1 sp, [ch 3, sc in next ch-1 sp] 4 times, ch 2, shell in shell, rep from * across, turn.

Row 11: Beg shell in shell, ch 2, sc in next ch-3 sp, [ch 3, sc in next ch-3 sp] 3 times, ch 2, shell in shell, *ch 1, shell in shell, ch 2, sc in next ch-3 sp, [ch 3, sc in next ch-3 sp] 3 times, ch 2, shell in shell, rep from * across, turn.

Row 12: Beg shell in shell, ch 2, sc in next ch-3 sp, [ch 3, sc in next ch-3 sp] twice, ch 2, shell in shell, *ch 2, dc in ch-1 sp, ch 2, shell in shell, ch 2, sc in next ch-3 sp, [ch 3, sc in next ch-3 sp] twice, ch 2, shell in shell, rep from * across, turn.

Row 13: Beg shell in shell, ch 2, sc in next ch-3 sp, ch 3, sc in next ch-3 sp, ch 2, shell in shell, *ch 2, V-st in single dc, ch 2, shell in shell, ch 2, sc in next ch-3 sp, ch 3, sc in next ch-3 sp, ch 2, shell in shell, rep from * across, turn.

Row 14: Beg shell in shell, ch 1, dc in ch-3 sp, ch 1, shell in shell, *ch 2, 6 dc in V-st, ch 2, shell in shell, ch 1, dc in ch-3 sp, ch 1, shell in shell, rep from * across, turn.

Rows 15–21: Rep rows 3–9.

PINEAPPLE FINISHING

Row 22 (RS): Beg shell in shell, ch 2, sc in next ch-1 sp, [ch 3, sc in next ch-1 sp] 4 times, ch 2, shell in shell, turn.

Row 23: Beg shell in shell, ch 2, sc in next ch-3 sp, [ch 3, sc in next ch-3 sp] 3 times, ch 2, shell in shell, turn.

Row 24: Beg shell in shell, ch 2, sc in next ch-3 sp, [ch 3, sc in next ch-3 sp] twice, ch 2, shell in shell, turn.

Row 25: Beg shell in shell, ch 2, sc in next ch-3 sp, ch 3, sc in next ch-3 sp, ch 2, shell in shell, turn.

Row 26: Beg shell in shell, ch 1, dc in next ch-3 sp, ch 1, shell in shell, turn.

Row 27: Beg shell in shell, shell in shell, turn.

Row 28: Sl st into ch-2 sp of shell, ch 1, sc in ch-2 sp of shell, ch 3, sc in next ch-2 sp of shell. Fasten off.

Next rows: *With finished pineapple to the right, join with sl st in next ch-2 sp of shell of row 21, rep rows 22–28. Rep from * until all 33 pineapples are completed across edge.

Top Trim
Row 1 (RS): Working in ch-4 sps created with first ball of cotton across opposite side of foundation ch of row 1 of Shower Curtain Valance, join with sl st in first ch-4 sp, ch 1, 3 sc in same ch sp, 3 sc in each of next 2 ch-4 sps, hold plastic ring in position behind next ch-4 sp, 3 sc over next ch-4 sp and ring, [3 sc over ring in each of next 16 ch-4 sps, hold next plastic ring in position behind next ch-4 sp, 3 sc over ring in next ch-4 sp and ring] 11 times, 3 sc over each of next 3 ch-4 sps. Fasten off. *(12 hanging rings across valance)*

Row 2 (RS): Join with sl st in first sc of previous row, ch 1, [sc in each sc to 3 sc over the plastic ring, work 15 sc over ring] across, ending with sc in each sc to end, turn.

Row 3 (WS): [Working across sc sts of row 2, sl st in each sc to just before ring, **do not sl st** around 15 sc of ring, instead sl st through 3 sts worked over ring in row 1] across. Fasten off.

Outer Edge Trim
Row 1 (WS): Join with sl st in end of row 2 of Top Trim, ch 1, sc in same row, ch 3, sc in starting ch, [ch 3, sc in end of next row] 27 times, *ch 3, (sc, ch 3, sc) in ch-3 sp of row 28 of pineapple, [ch 3, sc in end of next shell row] 6 times, ch 3, sc between shells of row 21, [ch 3, sc in end of next shell row] 6 times, rep from * across, ch 3, (sc, ch 3, sc) in ch-3 sp of row 28 of last pineapple, [ch 3, sc in end of next shell row] 27 times, ch 3, sc in foundation ch, ch 3, sc in end of row 2 of Top Trim, turn.

Row 2 (RS): Ch 1, (2 sc, ch 3, 2 sc) in each ch-3 sp across. Fasten off.

Starch and press valance.

Note: *Even though the Valance is 72 inches across, extra ribbon is needed for the weave.*

Cut 84-inch length of cream ribbon. Leaving a slight length at beg, weave through ch-4 sps of row 1 of Valance. Weave rem ends of ribbon through ch sps on WS; with sewing needle and thread, tack to secure.❑❑

Pineapple Bed Doll

Design by Agnes Russell

SKILL LEVEL
■■■□ INTERMEDIATE

FINISHED SIZE
10 inches tall

MATERIALS
- J. & P. Coats Old Fashioned crochet cotton size 10: 500 yds # 529 ecru
- Size 6/1.80mm steel crochet hook or size needed to obtain gauge
- Sharp tapestry needle
- Sewing needle
- Sewing thread:
  Ecru
  Teal
- 10-inch square teal chintz pillow with 3-inch ruffle
- 4 yds ¼-inch-wide teal satin ribbon
- 12 teal ½-inch ribbon roses
- 8-inch pillow doll by Fibre Craft
- 1-inch white button
- 2 snap fasteners
- Glue gun
- Spray starch

GAUGE
3 shell rnds = 1 inch

PATTERN NOTES
Both beginning shell and shell will be referred to as a shell; if round begins with a shell, simply work beginning shell, otherwise work a shell.

Both beginning double shell and double shell will be referred to as a double shell; if round begins with a double shell, simply work beginning double shell, otherwise work a double shell.

SPECIAL STITCHES
Beginning shell (beg shell): Sl st into ch-2 sp of shell, ch 3 *(counts as first dc)*, (dc, ch 2, 2 dc) in same ch-2 sp.

Shell: (2 dc, ch 2, 2 dc) in ch-2 sp of shell.

Beginning double shell (beg dbl shell): (Ch 3—*counts as first dc*, dc, ch 2, 2 dc, ch 2, 2 dc) in ch sp.

Double shell (dbl shell): (2 dc, ch 2, 2 dc, ch 2, 2 dc) in same ch-2 sp of shell.

INSTRUCTIIONS
DRESS
Bodice

Row 1 (WS): Starting at neckline, with ecru, ch 37, sc in second ch from hook and in each ch across, turn. *(36 sc)*

Row 2 (RS): Working in **back lps** *(see Stitch Guide)* for this row only, ch 1, sc in each st across, turn.

Row 3: Ch 3, sl st in first sc, [ch 3, sl st in next sc] across, turn.

Row 4: Ch 3, sl st in first ch-3 sp, [ch 3, sl st in next ch-3 sp] across, turn.

Row 5: Ch 3, sl st in first ch-3 sp, [ch 3, sl st in next ch-3 sp] across, turn. *(36 ch-3 sps)*

Row 6: Ch 1, 2 sc in each ch-3 sp across, turn. *(72 sc)*

Row 7: Ch 1, [sc in next sc, dc in next sc] 4 times, sc in next sc, (dc, sc, dc) in next sc, [sc in next sc, dc in next sc] 7 times, sc in next sc, (dc, sc, dc) in next sc, [sc in next sc, dc in next sc] 10 times, (sc, dc, sc) in next sc, [dc in next sc, sc in next sc] 7 times, dc in next sc, (sc, dc, sc) in next sc, [dc in next sc, sc in next dc] 4 times, dc in last sc, turn. *(80 sts)*

Row 8: Ch 1, [sc in next dc, dc in next sc] 5 times, (sc, dc, sc) in next dc, [dc in next sc, sc in next dc] 8 times, dc in next sc, (sc, dc, sc) in next dc, [dc in next sc, sc in next dc] 11 times, (dc, sc, dc) in next sc, [sc in next dc, dc in next sc] 8 times, sc in next dc, (dc, sc, dc) in next sc, [sc in next dc, dc in next sc] 5 times, turn. *(88 sts)*

Row 9: Ch 1, [sc in next dc, dc in next sc] 5 times, sc in next dc, (dc, sc, dc) in next sc, [sc in next dc, dc in next sc] 9 times, sc in next dc, (dc, sc, dc) in next sc, [sc in next dc, dc in next sc] 12 times, (sc, dc, sc) in next dc, [dc in next sc, sc in next dc] 9 times, dc in next sc, (sc, dc, sc) in next dc, [dc in next sc, sc in next dc] 5 times, dc in last sc, turn. *(96 sts)*

Row 10: Ch 1, [sc in next dc, dc in next sc] 6 times *(back)*, ch 2, sk next 22 sts *(armhole opening)*, [sc in next dc, dc in next sc] 14 times *(front)*, ch 2, sk next 22 sts *(armhole opening)*, [sc in next dc, dc in next sc] 6 times *(back)*, turn.

Row 11: Ch 1, [sc in next dc, dc in next sc] 6 times, sc in next ch, dc in next ch, [sc in next dc, dc in next sc] 14 times, sc in next ch, dc in next ch, [sc in next dc, dc in next sc] 6 times, turn. *(56 sts)*

Rows 12–17: Ch 1, [sc in next dc, dc in next sc] 28 times, turn.

Row 18 (RS): Ch 4 *(counts as first dc and ch 1)*, dc in next st, [ch 1, sk next st, dc in next st] across, turn. *(29 dc, 28 ch-1 sps)*

Row 19 (WS): Ch 1, sc in each dc and each ch-1 sp across, turn. *(57 sts)*

Row 20: Ch 1, working in back lps for this row only, sc in each st across, turn. *(57 sc)*

Row 21: Ch 1, sc in each of first 14 sts, 2 sc in next st, [sc in each of next 13 sts, 2 sc in next st] across, turn. *(61 sc)*

SKIRT

Row 22: Ch 5 *(counts as first dc and ch 2)*, dc in same st, [sk next 2 sc, (dc, ch 2, dc) in next sc] 20 times, turn.

Row 23: Beg shell *(see Special Stitches)* in first ch-2 sp, **shell** *(see Special Stitches)* in each ch-2 sp across, turn. *(21 shells)*

Row 24: Beg shell, [ch 2, shell in next ch-2 sp] 20 times, turn.

Row 25: Beg shell in first ch-2 sp, [ch 2, 6 dc in next ch-2 sp of shell, ch 2, shell in next shell] across, turn.

Row 26: Shell in shell *(see Pattern Note)*, *ch 2, dc in first dc of 6-dc group, [ch 1, dc in next dc] 5 times, ch 2, shell in shell, rep from * across, turn, sl st back into ch-2 sp of shell just completed.

Note: *The following steps will join skirt at center back.*

Rnd 27: Hold first shell of row 26 on top of last shell of row 26, insert hook through both ch-2 sps of shells, pull up lp, **beg dbl shell** *(see Special Stitches)* in same ch-2 sp, ch 2, sc in next ch-1 sp, [ch 3, sc in next ch-1 sp] 4 times, ch 2, *****dbl shell** *(see Special Stitches)* in shell, ch 2, sc in next ch-1 sp, [ch 3, sc in next ch-1 sp] 4 times, ch 2, rep from * around, join with sl st in top of beg ch-3.

Rnd 28: *[Shell in shell, ch 2] twice, sc in next ch-3 sp, [ch 3, sc in next ch-3 sp] 3 times, ch 2, rep from * around, join.

Rnd 29: *Shell in shell, ch 2, dc in ch-2 sp between shells, ch 2, shell in shell, ch 2, sc in next ch-3 sp, [ch 3, sc in next ch-3 sp] 2 times, ch 2, rep from * around, join.

Rnd 30: *Shell in shell, ch 2, shell in single dc between shells, ch 2, shell in shell, ch 2, sc in next ch-3 sp, ch 3, sc in next ch-3 sp, ch 2, rep from * around, join.

Rnd 31: *Shell in shell, ch 2, 8 dc in next ch-2 sp of shell, ch 2, shell in shell, ch 2, sc in next ch-3 sp, ch 2, rep from * around, join.

Rnd 32: *Shell in shell, ch 2, dc in next dc of 8-dc group, [ch 1, dc in next dc] 7 times, ch 2, shell in shell, ch 2, rep from * around, join.

Rnd 33: *Shell in shell, ch 2, sc in next ch-1 sp, [ch 3, sc in next ch-1 sp] 6 times, ch 2, shell in shell, ch 2, dc in ch-2 sp between shells, ch 2, rep from * around, join.

Rnd 34: *Shell in shell, ch 2, sc in next ch-3 sp, [ch 3, sc in next ch-3 sp] 5 times, ch 2, shell in shell, ch 2, (dc, ch 3, dc) in single dc between shells, ch 2, rep from * around, join.

Rnd 35: *Shell in shell, ch 2, sc in next ch-3 sp, [ch 3, sc in next ch-3 sp] 4 times, ch 2, shell in shell, ch 2, shell in ch-3 sp between 2 dc sts, ch 2, rep from * around, join.

Rnd 36: *Beg dbl shell in shell, ch 2, sc in next ch-3 sp, [ch 3, sc in next ch-3 sp] 3 times, ch 2, dbl shell in shell, ch 2, shell in shell, ch 2, rep from * around, join.

Rnd 37: *[Shell in shell, ch 2] twice, sc in next ch-3 sp, [ch 3, sc in next ch-3 sp] 2 times, ch 2, [shell in shell, ch 2] 3 times, rep from * around, join.

Rnd 38: *[Shell in shell, ch 2] twice, sc in next ch-3 sp, ch 3, sc in next ch-3 sp, ch 2, [shell in shell, ch 2] 3 times, rep from * around, join.

Rnd 39: *Shell in shell, ch 2, dc in ch-2 sp between shells, ch 2, shell in shell, ch 2, dc in next ch-3 sp, ch 2, shell in shell, ch 2, dc in next ch-2 sp between shells, ch 2, [shell in shell, ch 2] twice, rep from * around, join.

Rnd 40: Sl st into ch-2 sp of shell, ch 6 *(counts as first dc and ch 3)*, *[dc in next ch-2 sp, ch 3] 3 times, dc in next dc at top of pineapple, sk next ch-2 sp, ch 3, [dc in next ch-2 sp, ch 3] 8 times, rep from * around, join with sl st in third ch of beg ch-6.

Rnd 41: Sl st into ch-3 sp, ch 4 *(counts as first dc and ch 1)*, [dc, ch 1] 7 times in same ch-3 sp, *[dc, ch 1] 8 times in next ch-3 sp, rep from * around, join with sl st in third ch of beg ch-4.

Rnd 42: Sl st into ch-1 sp, ch 1, sc in same ch-1 sp, ch 4, [sc in next ch-1 sp, ch 4] around, join with sl st in beg sc.

Rnd 43: Sl st into ch-4 sp, ch 1, (sc, ch 3, sc) in same ch-4 sp, (sc, ch 3, sc) in each ch-4 sp around, join. Fasten off.

WAISTLINE TRIM

Join ecru with sl st in rem free lp of row 19, ch 1, (sc, ch 3, sc) in same st, [sk next st, (sc, ch 3, sc) in next st] across. Fasten off.

LEFT BACK TRIM
Row 1: Join ecru with sl st in end of row 18, ch 1, work 23 sc evenly sp up back opening, turn. *(23 sc)*
Row 2: Ch 1, sc in each next 23 sc. Fasten off.

RIGHT BACK TRIM
Row 1: Join ecru with sl st at neck edge, ch 1, working down back across rows 1–18, work 23 sc evenly sp, turn.
Row 2: Ch 1, sc in each next 23 sc. Fasten off.

BODICE TRIM
Row 1: Join ecru with sl st in rem free lp of row 1, ch 1, sc in same st, [ch 3, sc in next st] across, turn.
Row 2: Ch 1, (sc, ch 3, sc) in each ch-3 sp across. Fasten off.

NECKLINE TRIM
Row 1: Working in starting ch on opposite side of row 1, join ecru with sl st in first ch, ch 1, sc in each ch across, turn.
Row 2: Sl st tightly in each sc across. Fasten off.

SLEEVE
Make 2.
Rnd 1 (RS): Join ecru with sl st in first ch of underarm, ch 1, sc in same ch, dc in next ch, [sc in next dc, dc in next sc] 11 times, join with sl st in beg sc, turn. *(24 sts)*
Rnds 2–6: Ch 1, [sc in next dc, dc in next sc] 12 times, join, turn.
Rnd 7 (RS): Ch 4 *(counts as first dc and ch 1)*, sk next st, [dc in next st, ch 1, sk next st] around, join with sl st in third ch of beg ch-4.
Rnd 8 (RS): Sl st into ch-1 sp, ch 1, sc in same ch sp, ch 3, [sc in next ch-1 sp, ch 3] around, join.
Rnd 9: Sl st into ch-3 sp, ch 1, (sc, ch 3, sc) in same ch-3 sp, (sc, ch 3, sc) in each ch-3 sp around, join. Fasten off.

DRESS FINISHING
1. Lightly starch and press Dress. With sewing needle and ecru sewing thread, sew snap fasteners to back opening.
2. Cut a 25-inch length of ribbon and starting at center back, weave through ch-2 sps of row 18 of Dress. Tie ends in a large bow at center back.
3. Cut five lengths of ribbon each 9 inches long. Tie each length of ribbon around ribbon rose in a bow just below base of flower on stem.
4. Cut stem from ribbon rose ¼ inch below tied ribbon.
5. Glue one ribboned rose to every other dc at point of pineapple on rnd 39.
6. Cut two lengths of ribbon each 12 inches long. Weave each length through ch-1 sps of rnd 7 of each Sleeve. Tie ends in a bow.
7. Cut stem off one rose. Glue rose to center front of bodice at neckline.
8. Glue six roses to right hand.

PILLOW
With sewing needle and double strand of teal thread, working around square corners at base of ruffle to round off edges, weave thread in gathering st 4 inches before and after corner, pull gently to round off corner, knot to secure. Rep on each corner.

BUTTON
Rnd 1: With ecru, ch 2, 5 sc in second ch from hook, join with sl st in beg sc. *(5 sc)*
Rnd 2: Ch 3, dc in same st, 2 dc in each sc around, join with sl st in top of beg ch-3. *(10 dc)*
Rnd 3: Ch 3, dc in same st, 2 dc in each dc around, join. *(20 dc)*
Rnd 4: Ch 3, dc in each dc around, join.
Rnd 5: Ch 1, sc in each st around, join. Leaving long end, fasten off.
Thread needle with long end, weave through sts of rnd 5, pull slightly to gather, insert button, pull to close, sew and knot opening closed.

CHAIN
With one strand ecru, ch 150. Leaving long end, fasten off.
Thread long end into sharp yarn needle, insert needle through center top of pillow and out bottom, insert needle through one hole of button and then back through another hole, back through center of pillow to starting point. Pull ends of chain at top of pillow, indenting center of pillow completely, knot ends tog to secure.
Insert pillow chain through bottom lp on doll body, tie ends in a bow.
Place Dress on doll.

HAIR RIBBON
Note: *For best results with hair ribbon, place doll's hair in a ponytail or bun.*

FIRST HALF
Row 1: With ecru, ch 32, (dc, ch 2, 2 dc) in fourth ch from hook, [ch 2, sk next 6 chs, shell in next ch] 4 times, turn, sl st into ch-2 sp of shell.
Row 2: Shell in ch-2 sp, [ch 2, 6 dc in next ch-2 sp of shell, ch 2, shell in ch-2 sp of shell] twice, turn.
Row 3: Shell in ch-2 sp, *ch 2, dc in first dc of 6-dc group, [ch 1, dc in next dc] 5 times, ch 2, shell in shell, rep from * once, turn.
Row 4: Shell in ch-2 sp of shell, *ch 2, sc in next ch-1 sp, [ch 3, sc in next ch-1 sp] 4 times, ch 2, shell in shell, rep from * once, turn.
Row 5: Shell in ch-2 sp, *ch 2, sc in next ch-3 sp, [ch 3, sc in next ch-3 sp] 3 times, ch 2, shell in shell, rep from * once, turn.
Row 6: Shell in ch-2 sp, *ch 2, sc in next ch-3 sp, [ch 3, sc in next ch-3 sp] 2 times, ch 2, shell in shell, rep from * once, turn.
Row 7: Shell in ch-2 sp, *ch 2, sc in next ch-3 sp, ch 3, sc in next ch-3 sp, ch 2, shell in shell, rep from * once, turn.
Row 8: Shell in ch-2 sp of shell, *ch 2, dc in next ch-3 sp, ch 2, shell in shell, rep from * once, turn.
Row 9: Shell in ch-2 sp of shell, *ch 2, (dc, ch 2, dc) in single dc at top of pineapple, ch 2, shell in shell, rep from * once, turn.

Row 10: Shell in ch-2 sp of shell, *ch 2, shell in ch-2 sp between dc sts at top of pineapple, ch 2, shell in ch-2 sp of shell, rep from * once, turn.

Rows 11–19: Rep rows 2–10.

Rows 20 & 21: Rep rows 2 and 3.

Row 22: Shell in shell, ch 2, sc in next ch-1 sp, [ch 3, sc in next ch-1 sp] 4 times, ch 2, double shell in next ch-2 sp of shell, ch 2, sc in next ch-1 sp, [ch 3, sc in next ch-1 sp] 4 times, ch 2, shell in shell, turn.

FIRST PINEAPPLE FINISHING

Row 23: Shell in shell, ch 2, sc in next ch-3 sp, [ch 3, sc in next ch-3 sp] 3 times, ch 2, shell in shell, turn.

Row 24: Shell in shell, ch 2, sc in next ch-3 sp, [ch 3, sc in next ch-3 sp] 2 times, ch 2, shell in shell, turn.

Row 25: Shell in shell, ch 2, sc in next ch-3 sp, ch 3, sc in next ch-3 sp, ch 2, shell in shell, turn.

Row 26: Shell in shell, dc in ch-3 sp, shell in shell. Fasten off.

SECOND PINEAPPLE FINISHING

Row 23: With WS of row 22 facing, finished pineapple to the right, join ecru with sl st in next ch-2 sp of shell, ch 3, (dc, ch 2, 2 dc) in same ch-2 sp, ch 2, sc in next ch-3 sp, [ch 3, sc in next ch-3 sp] 3 times, ch 2, shell in shell, turn.

Rows 24–26: Rep rows 24–26 of First Pineapple Finishing.

SECOND HALF

Row 1 (RS): With row 1 of First Half facing and working on opposite side of foundation ch, join ecru with sl st in same ch as first shell, beg shell in same ch, [sk next 6 chs, shell in same ch as next shell on First Half] 4 times, turn.

Rows 2–22: Rep rows 2–22 of First Half.

FIRST PINEAPPLE FINISHING

Rows 23–26: Rep rows 23–26 of First Pineapple Finishing.

SECOND PINEAPPLE FINISHING

Rows 23–26: Rep rows 23–26 of Second Pineapple Finishing.

FINISHING

1. Lightly starch and press Hair Ribbon.
2. Cut two lengths each 20 inches and two lengths each 5 inches.
3. With first 20-inch length of ribbon, weave through ch sps of shells on outer edge. Weave second 20-inch length through ch sps on opposite outer edge of shells.
4. Weave each rem 5-inch length through inner shell sps at each end of pineapple finishing.
5. Fold each end of ribbon under and glue to secure. Trim any excess ribbon.
6. Fold Hair Ribbon lengthwise so that outer ribbons woven through end shells are showing, wrap around hair and tie in place. Fan out end pineapples.❑❑

306 East Parr Road
Berne, IN 46711
© 2005 Annie's Attic

TOLL-FREE ORDER LINE or to request a free catalog (800) LV-ANNIE (800) 582-6643
Customer Service (800) AT-ANNIE (800) 282-6643, **Fax** (800) 882-6643
Visit www.AnniesAttic.com

We have made every effort to ensure the accuracy and completeness of these instructions. We cannot, however, be responsible for human error, typographical mistakes or variations in individual work. Reprinting or duplicating the information, photographs or graphics in this publication by any means, including copy machine, computer scanning, digital photography, e-mail, personal Web site and fax, is illegal. Failure to abide by federal copyright laws may result in litigation and fines.

ISBN: 1-59635-026-1   All rights reserved.   Printed in USA

Stitch Guide

ABBREVIATIONS

beg	begin/beginning
bpdc	back post double crochet
bpsc	back post single crochet
bptr	back post treble crochet
CC	contrasting color
ch	chain stitch
ch-	refers to chain or space previously made (i.e. ch-1 space)
ch sp	chain space
cl	cluster
cm	centimeter(s)
dc	double crochet
dec	decrease/decreases/decreasing
dtr	double treble crochet
fpdc	front post double crochet
fpsc	front post single crochet
fptr	front post treble crochet
g	gram(s)
hdc	half double crochet
inc	increase/increases/increasing
lp(s)	loop(s)
MC	main color
mm	millimeter(s)
oz	ounce(s)
pc	popcorn
rem	remain/remaining
rep	repeat(s)
rnd(s)	round(s)
RS	right side
sc	single crochet
sk	skip(ped)
sl st	slip stitch
sp(s)	space(s)
st(s)	stitch(es)
tog	together
tr	treble crochet
trtr	triple treble
WS	wrong side
yd(s)	yard(s)
yo	yarn over

Chain—ch: Yo, pull through lp on hook.

Slip stitch—sl st: Insert hook in st, yo, pull through both lps on hook.

Single crochet—sc: Insert hook in st, yo, pull through st, yo, pull through both lps on hook.

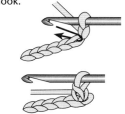

Front loop—front lp
Back loop—back lp

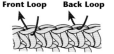

Front post stitch—fp: Back post stitch—bp: When working post st, insert hook from right to left around post st on previous row.

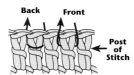

Half double crochet—hdc: Yo, insert hook in st, yo, pull through st, yo, pull through all 3 lps on hook.

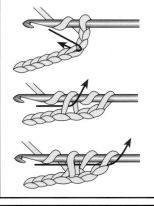

Double crochet—dc: Yo, insert hook in st, yo, pull through st, [yo, pull through 2 lps] twice.

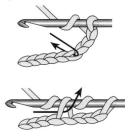

Change colors: Drop first color; with second color, pull through last 2 lps of st.

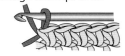

Treble crochet—tr: Yo twice, insert hook in st, yo, pull through st, [yo, pull through 2 lps] 3 times.

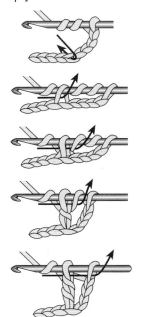

Double treble crochet—dtr: Yo 3 times, insert hook in st, yo, pull through st, [yo, pull through 2 lps] 4 times.

Single crochet decrease (sc dec): (Insert hook, yo, draw up a lp) in each of the sts indicated, yo, draw through all lps on hook.

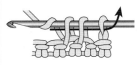
Example of 2-sc dec

Half double crochet decrease (hdc dec): (Yo, insert hook, yo, draw lp through) in each of the sts indicated, yo, draw through all lps on hook.

Example of 2-hdc dec

Double crochet decrease (dc dec): (Yo, insert hook, yo, draw lp through, yo, draw through 2 lps on hook) in each of the sts indicated, yo, draw through all lps on hook.

Example of 2-dc dec

US		UK
sl st (slip stitch)	=	sc (single crochet)
sc (single crochet)	=	dc (double crochet)
hdc (half double crochet)	=	htr (half treble crochet)
dc (double crochet)	=	tr (treble crochet)
tr (treble crochet)	=	dtr (double treble crochet)
dtr (double treble crochet)	=	ttr (triple treble crochet)
skip	=	miss

For more complete information, visit

StitchGuide.com